TATTOO

COLORING BOOK FOR MEN AND WOMEN

THIS BOOK BELONGS TO

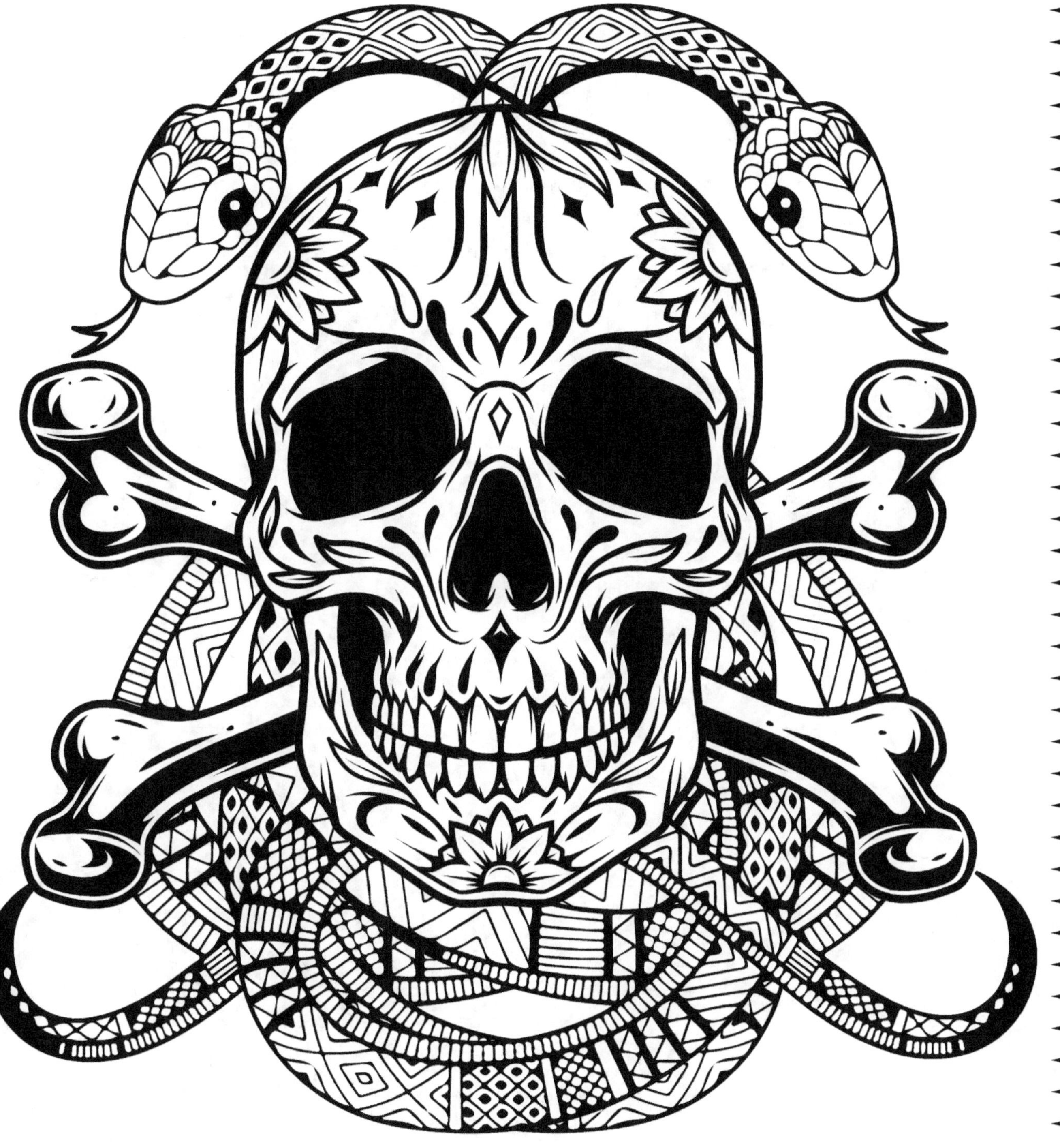

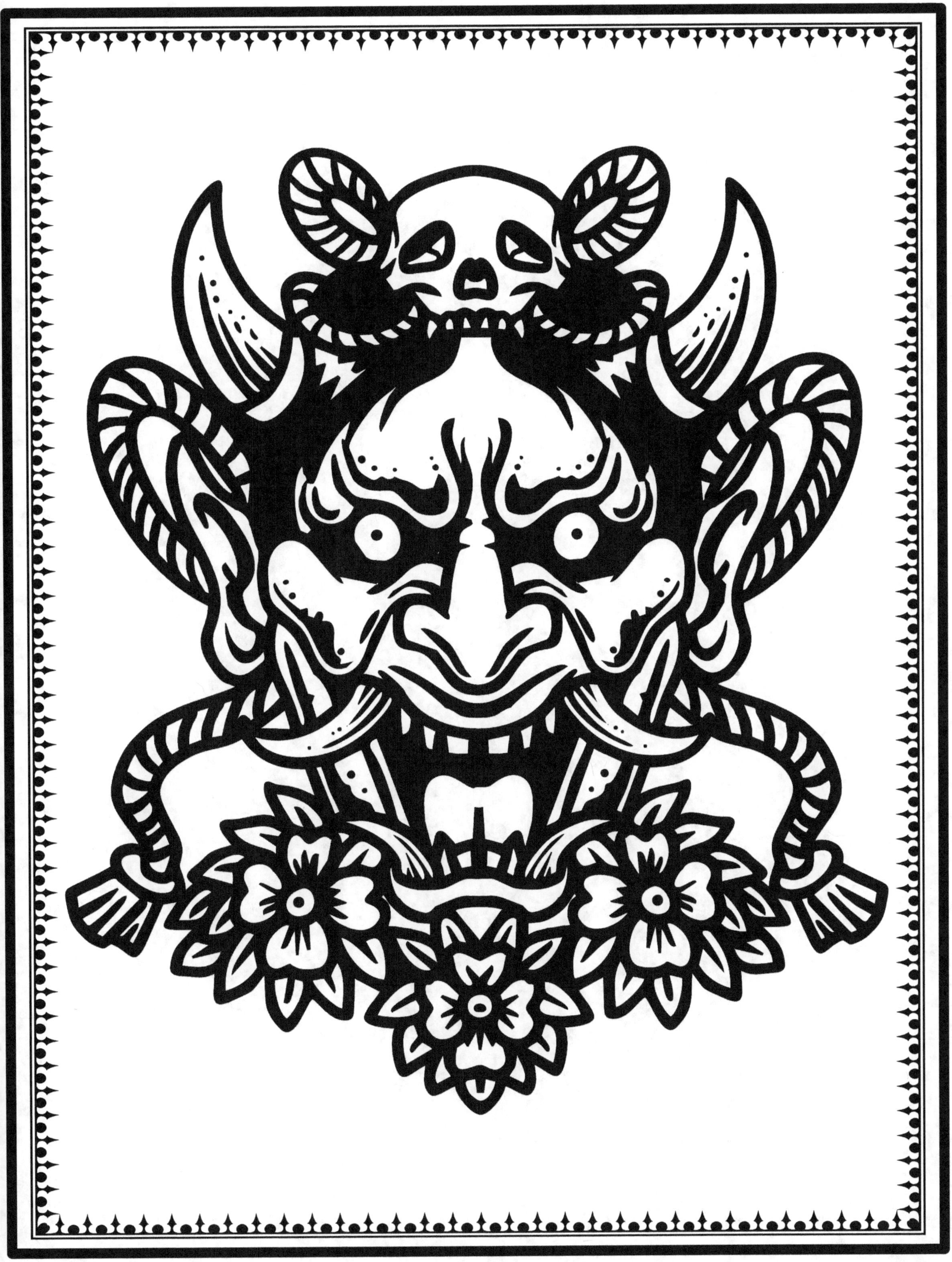

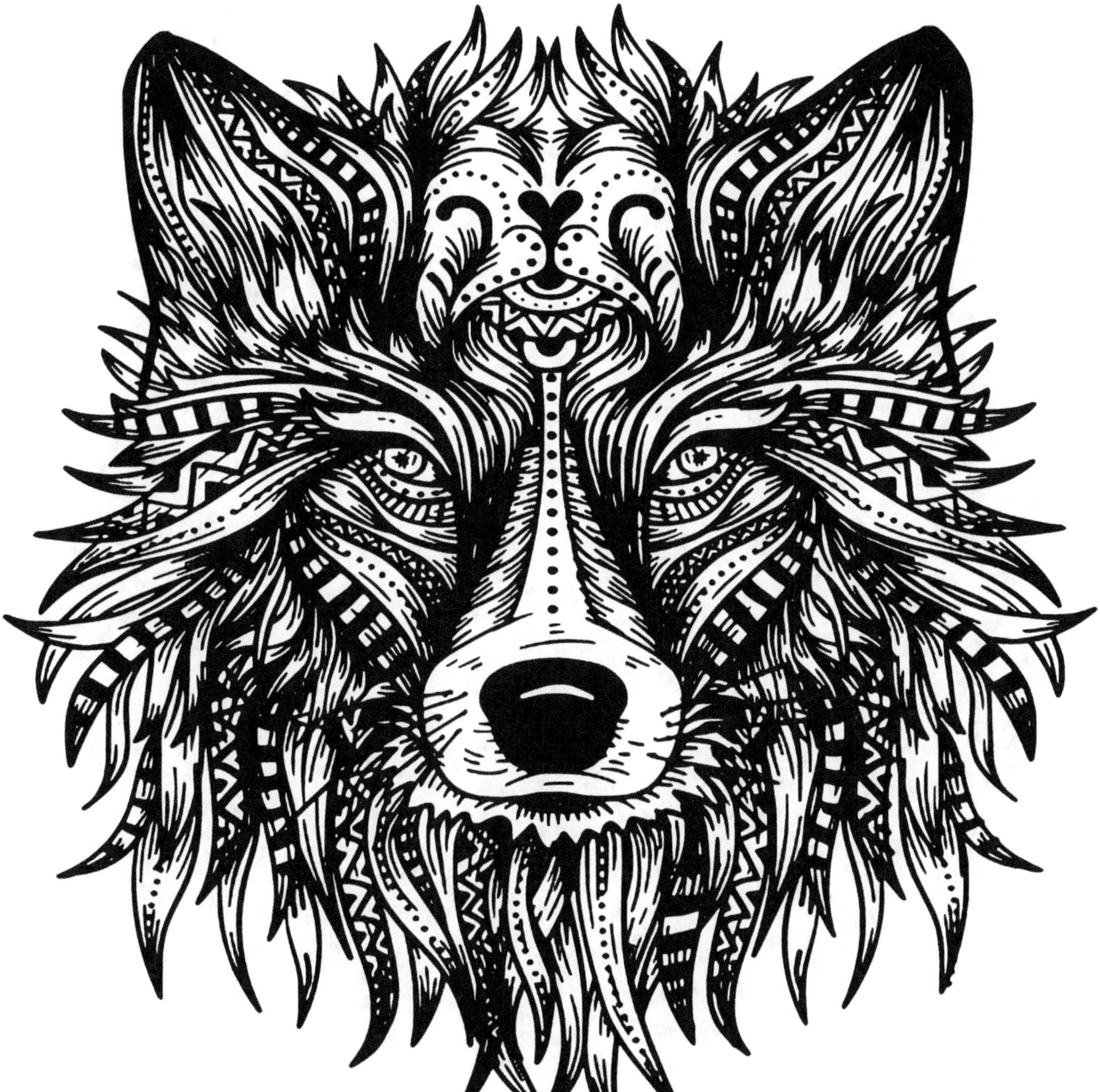

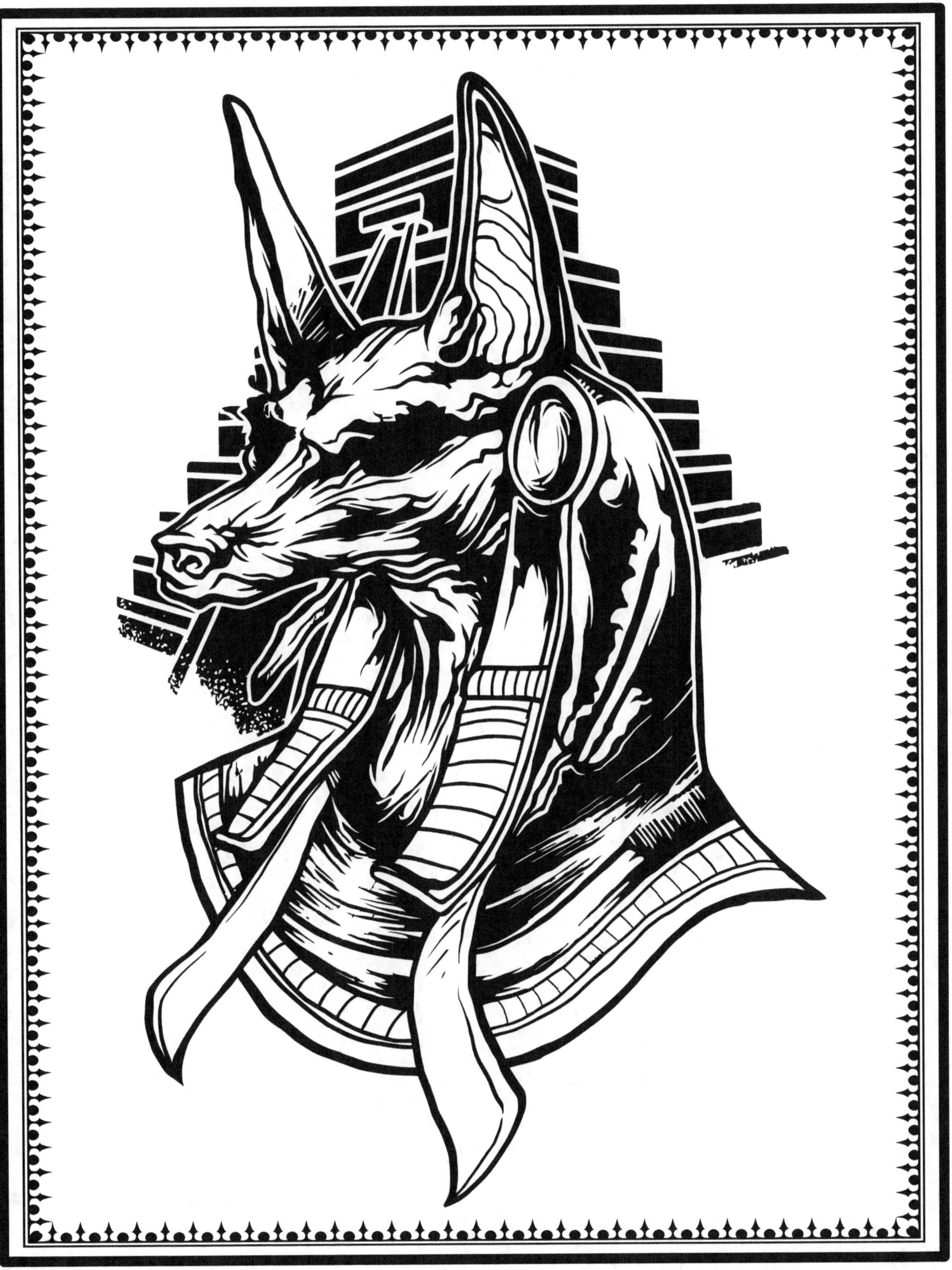

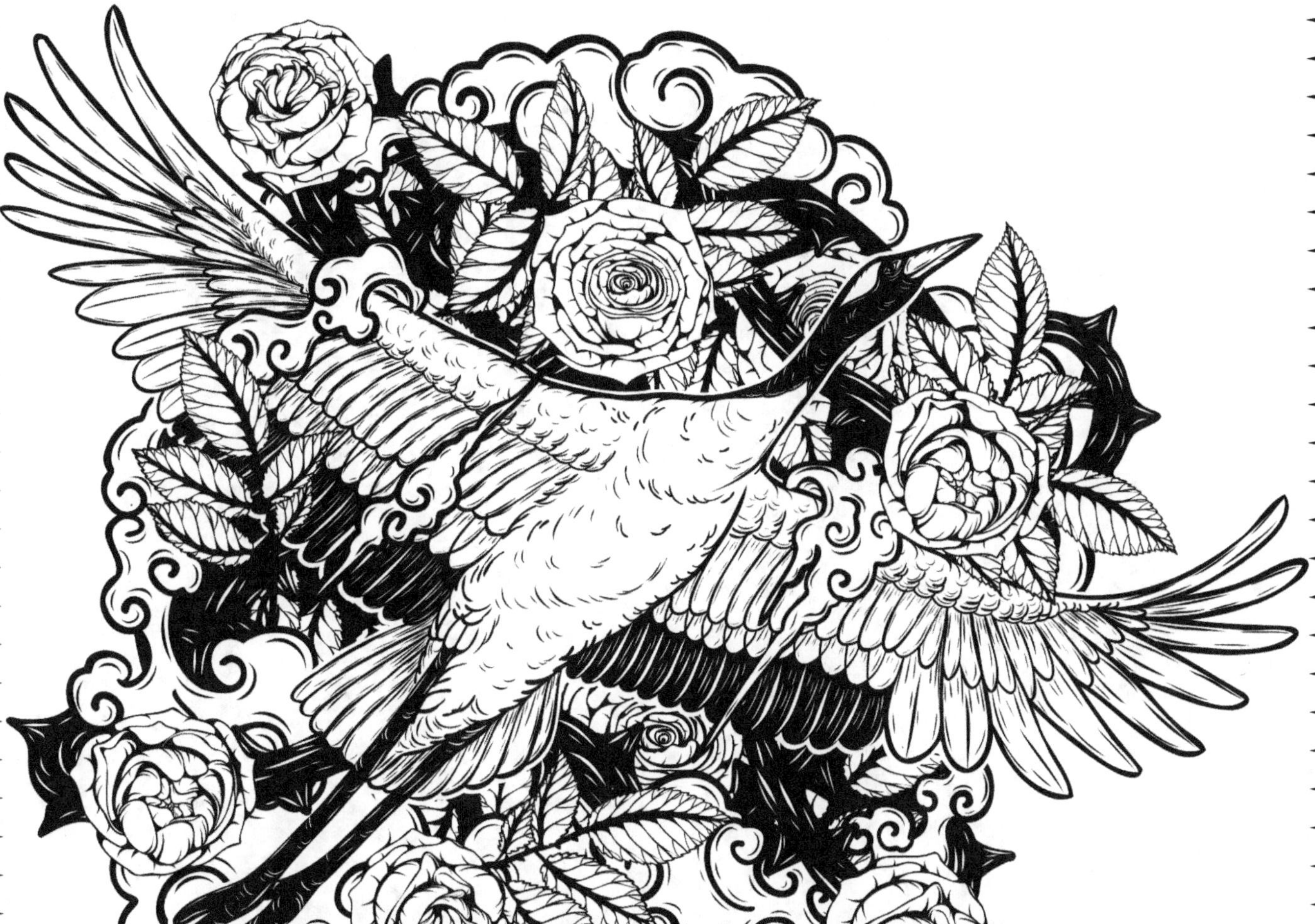

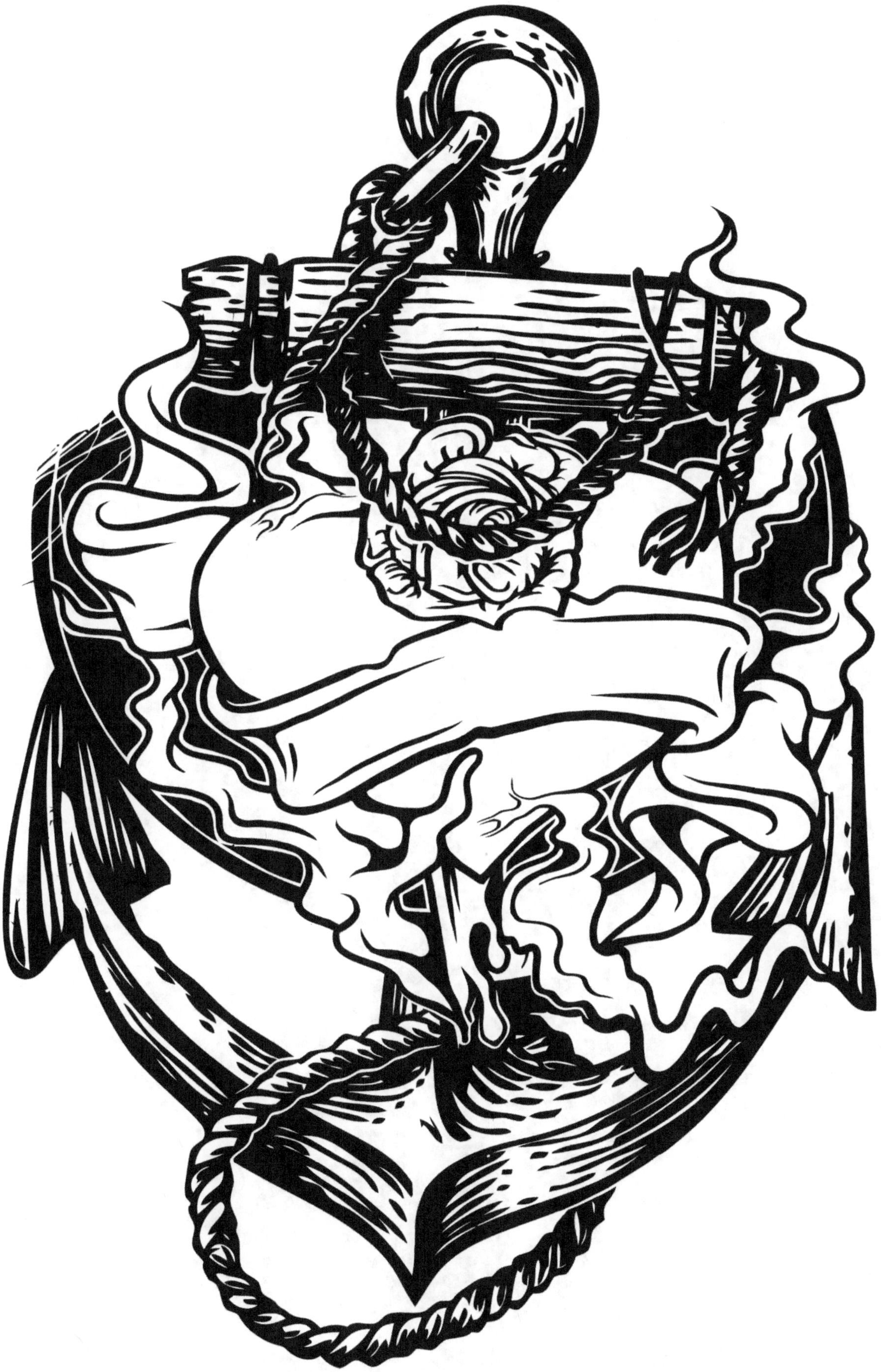

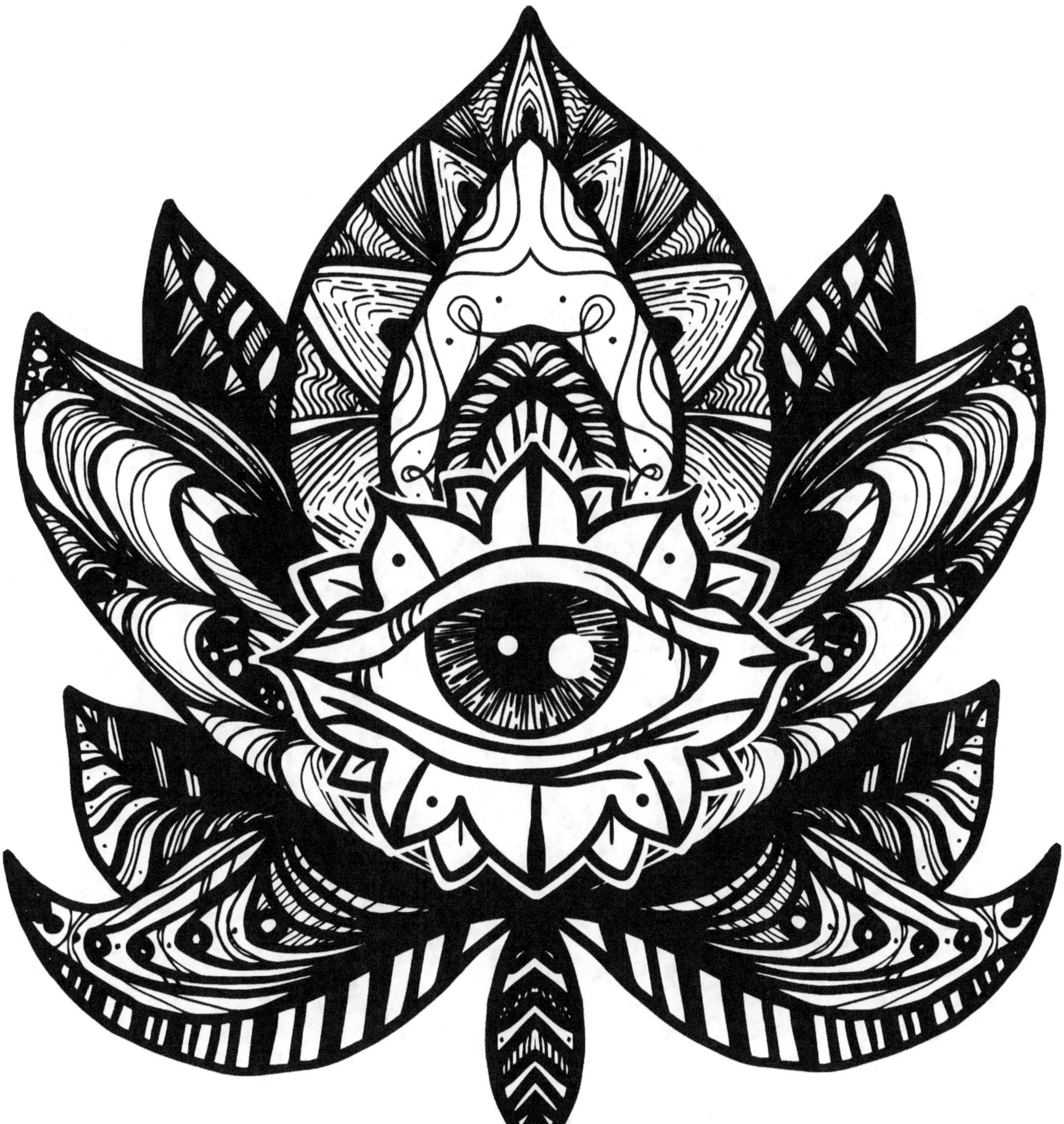

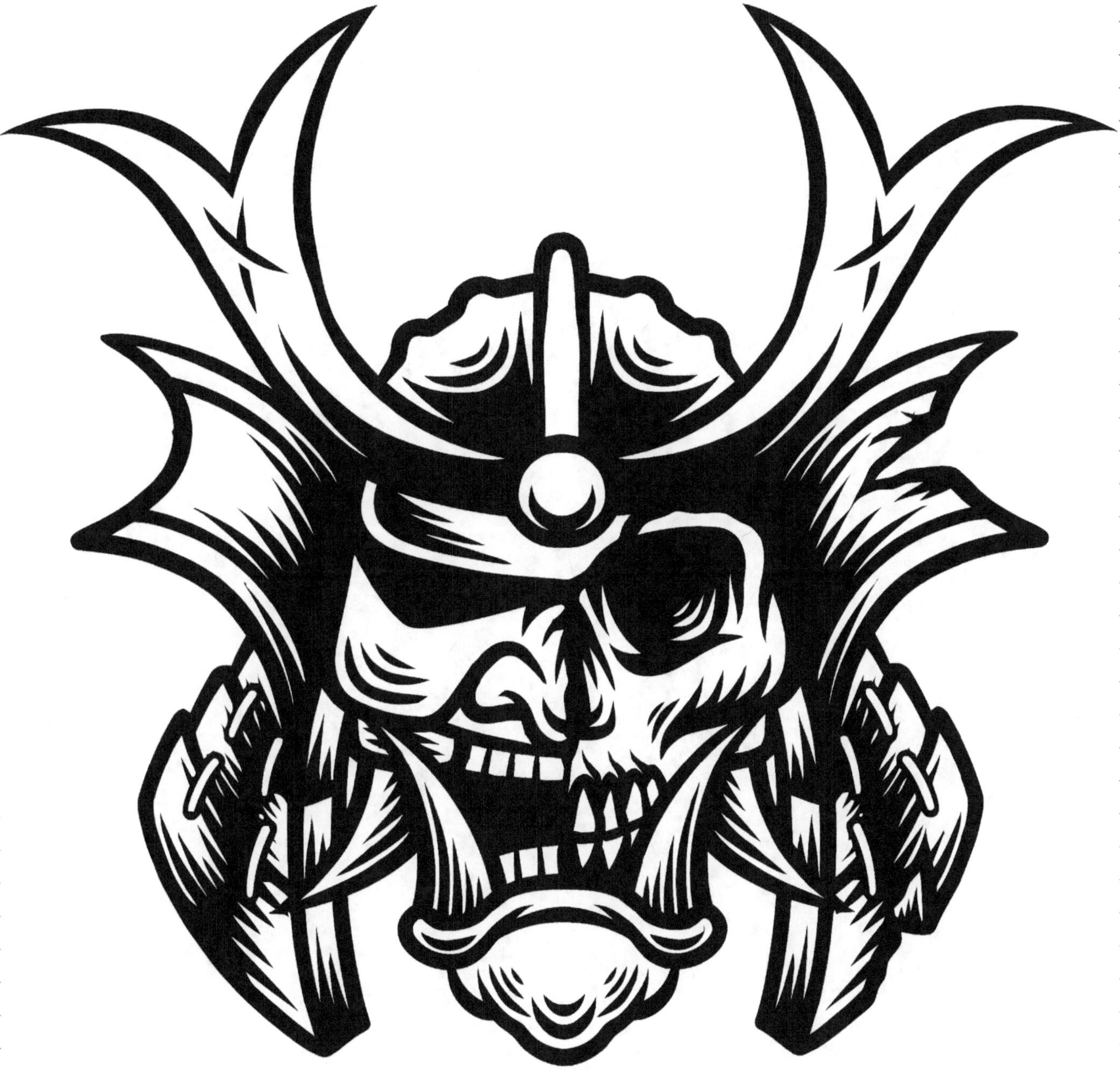

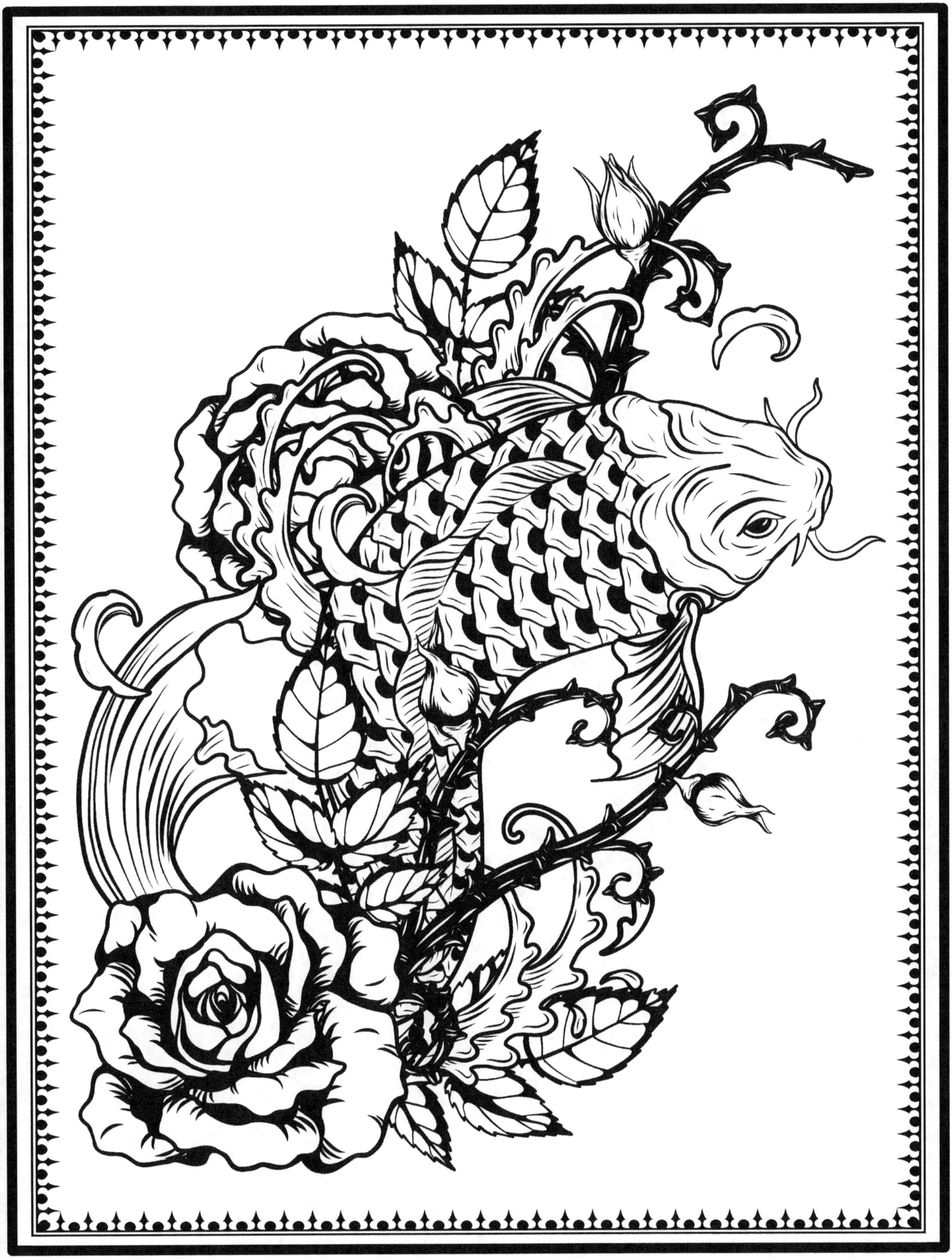

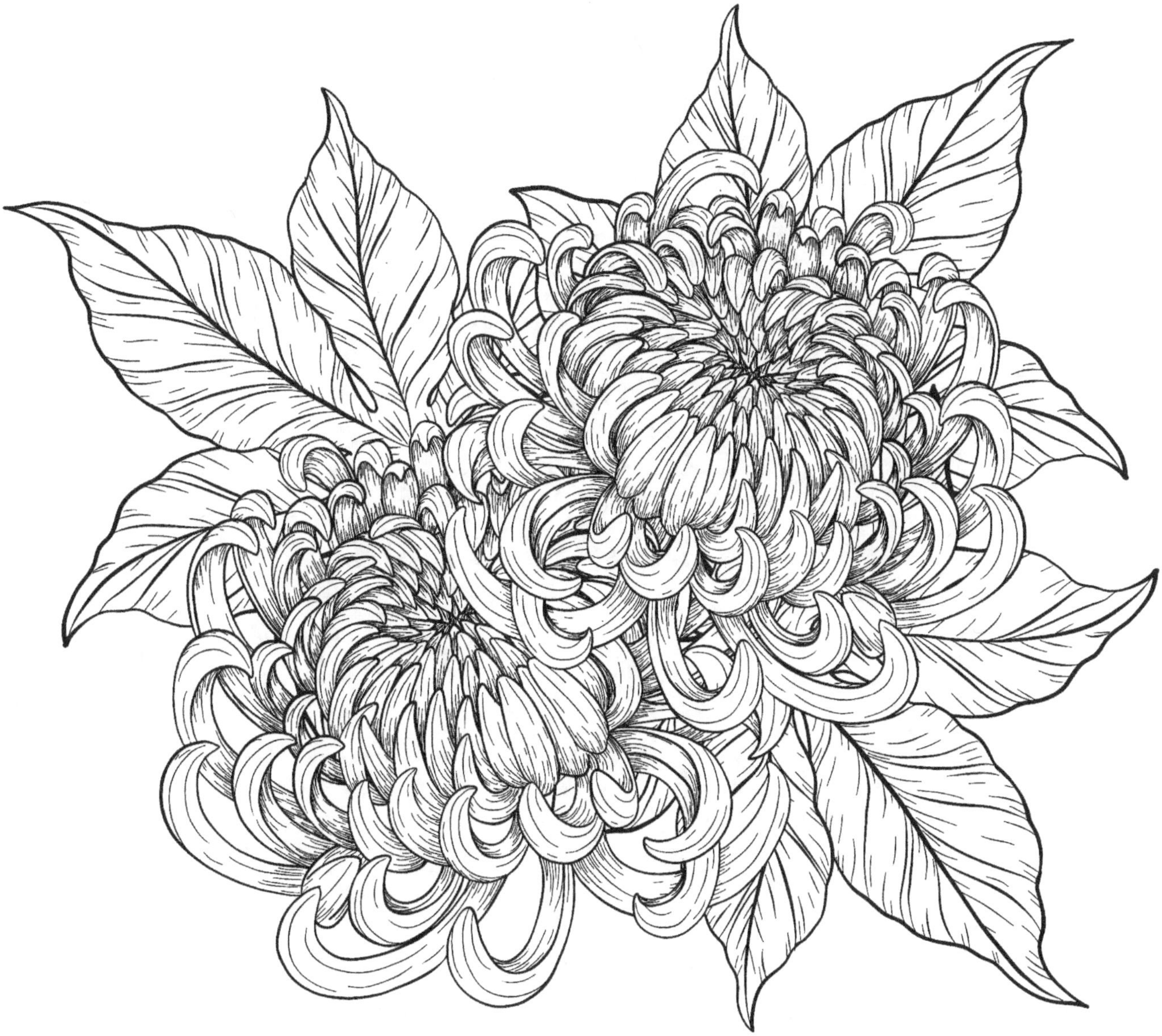

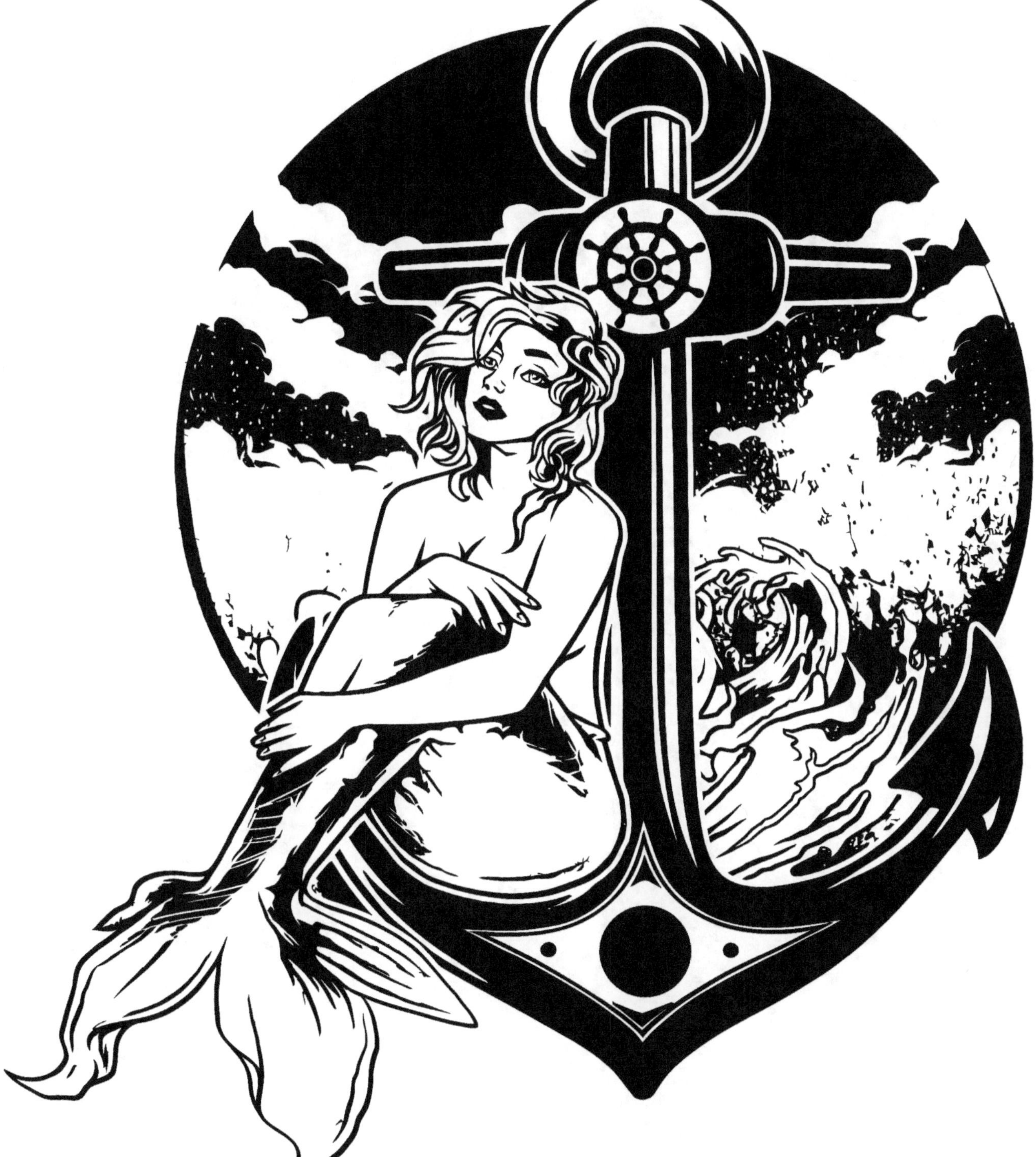

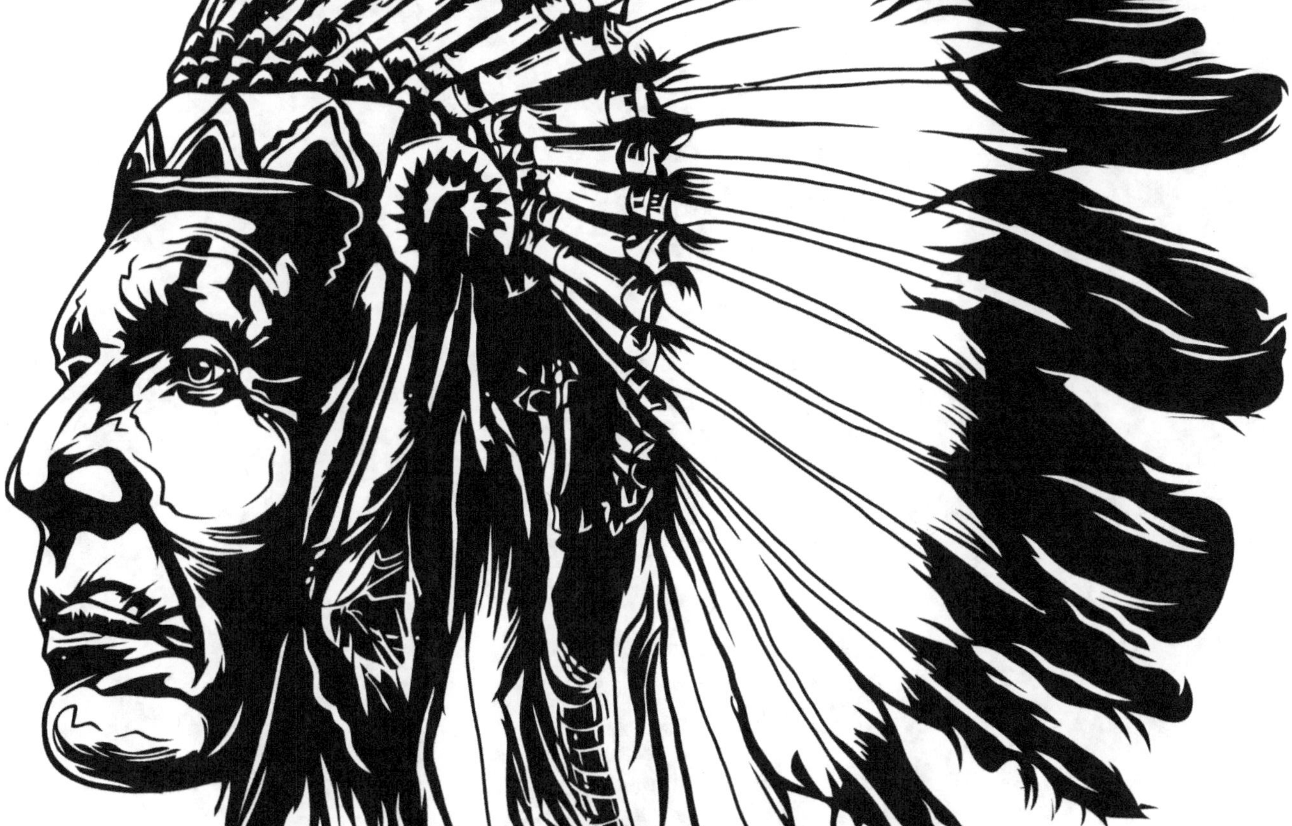

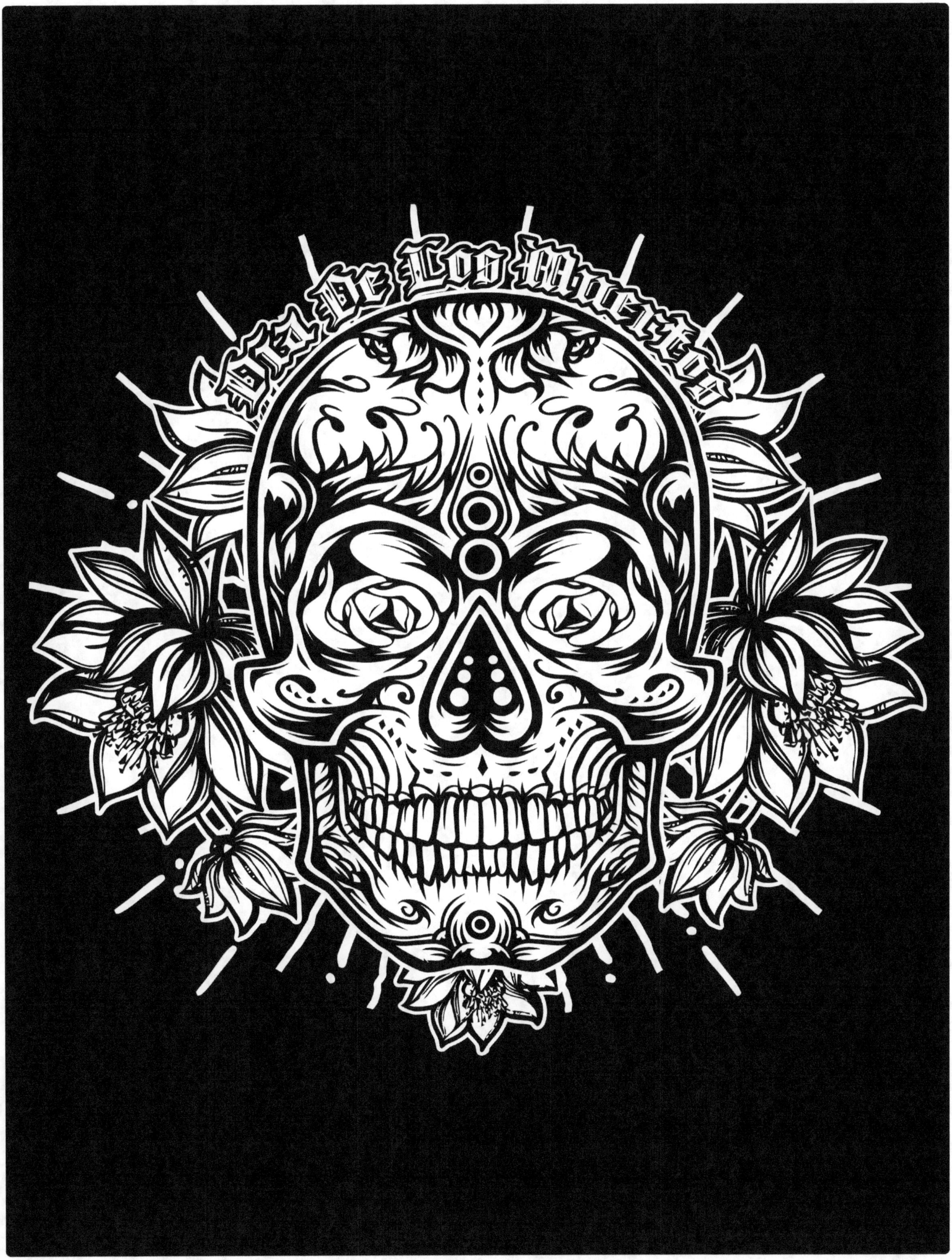
Dia De Los Muertos

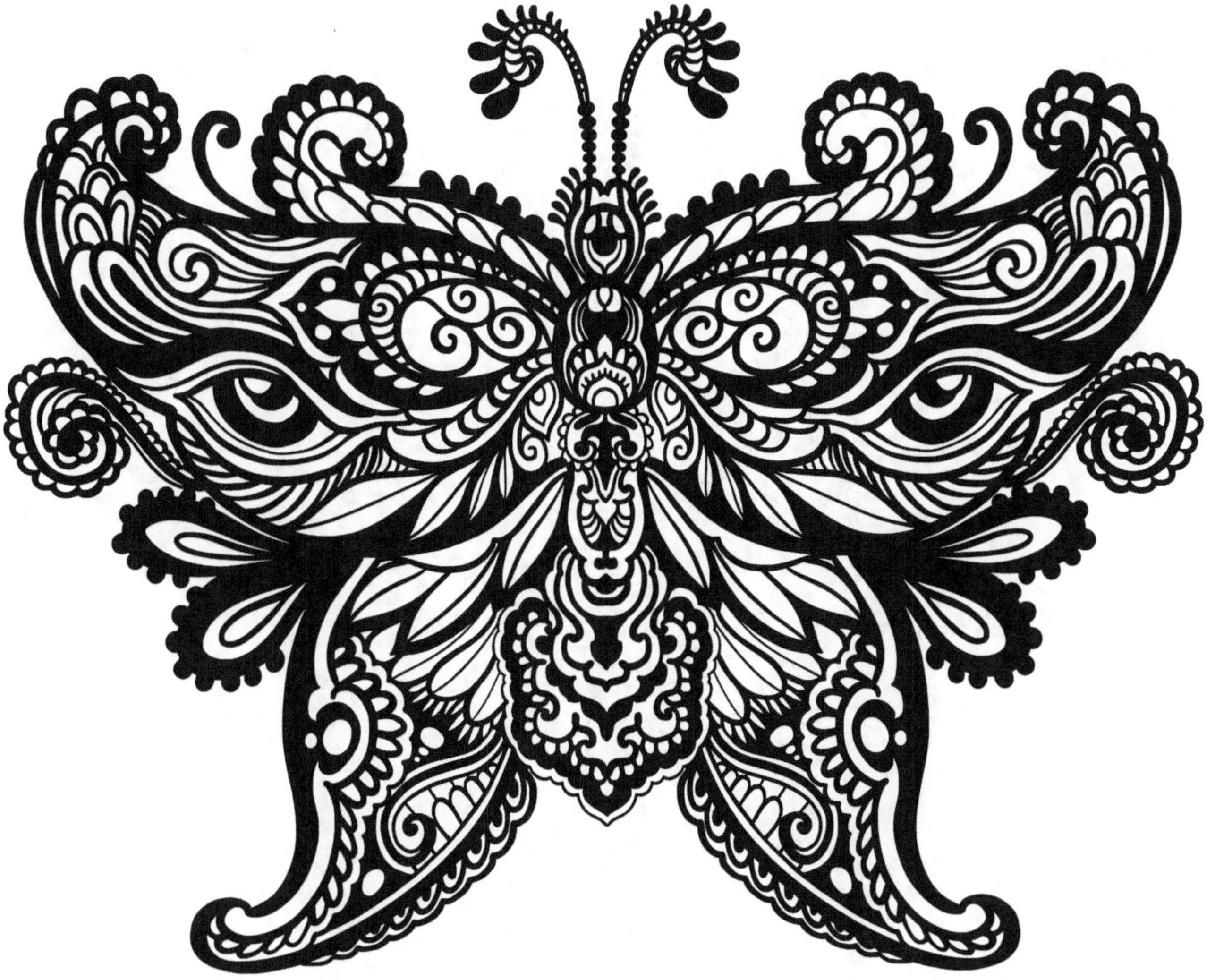

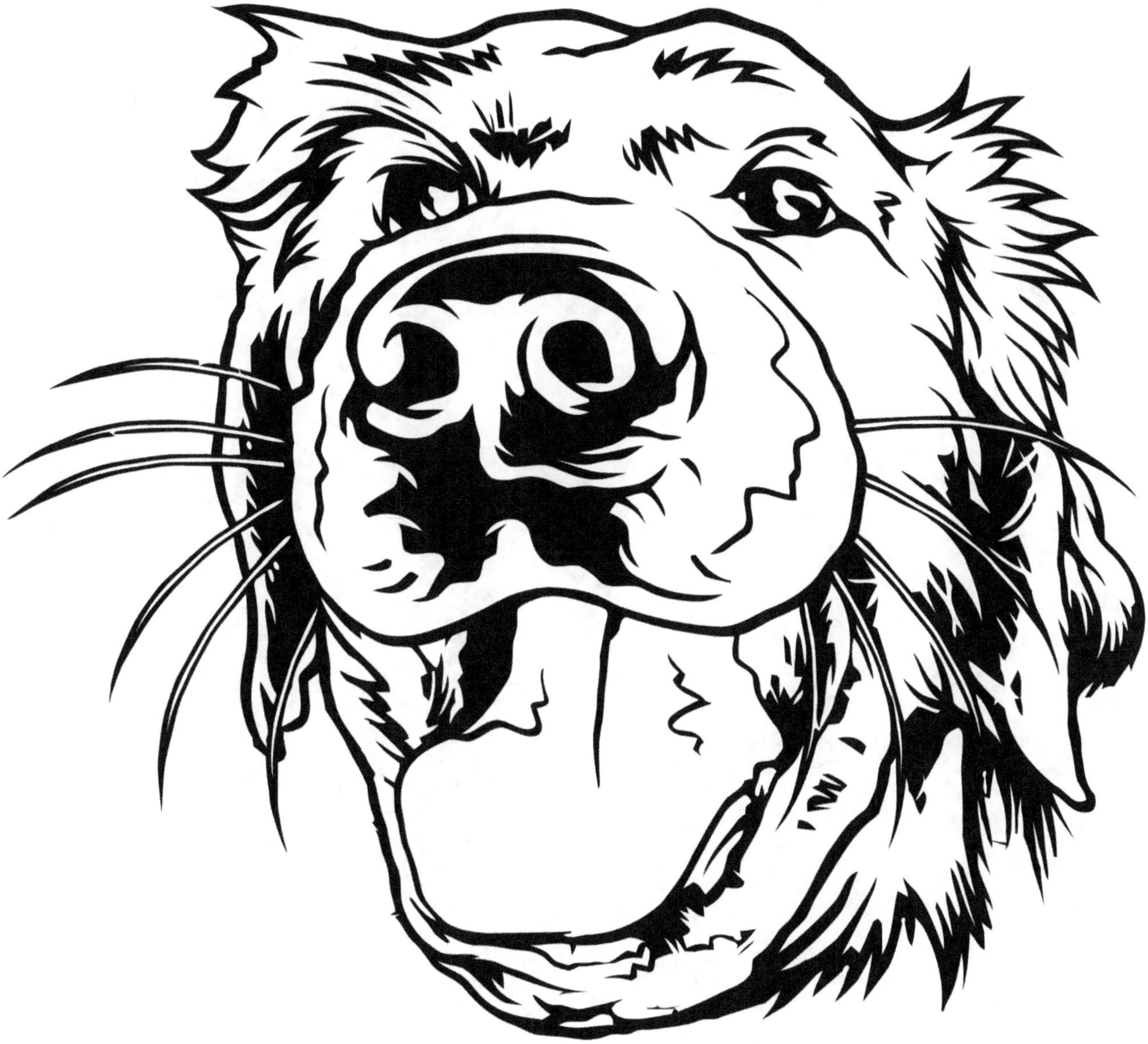

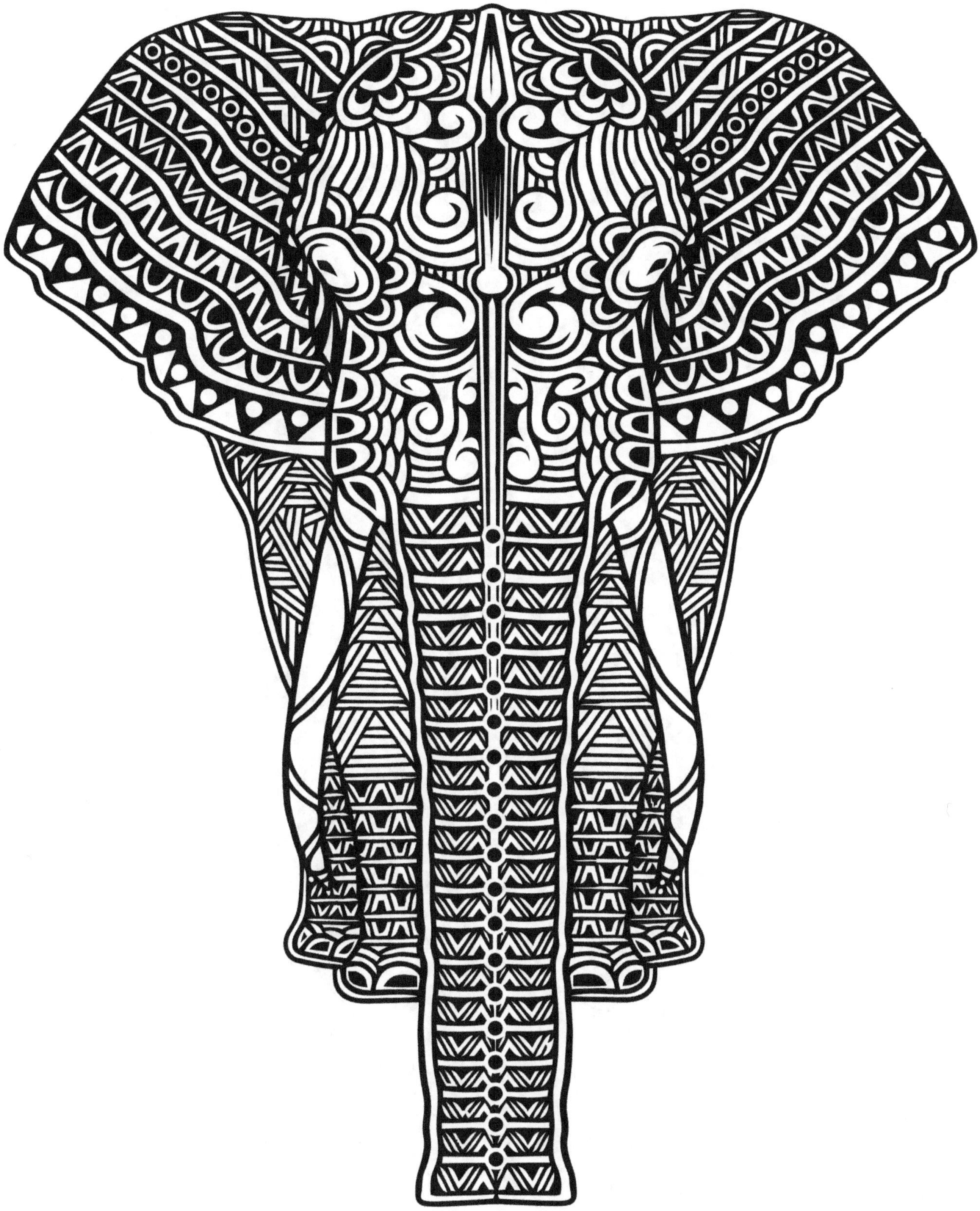

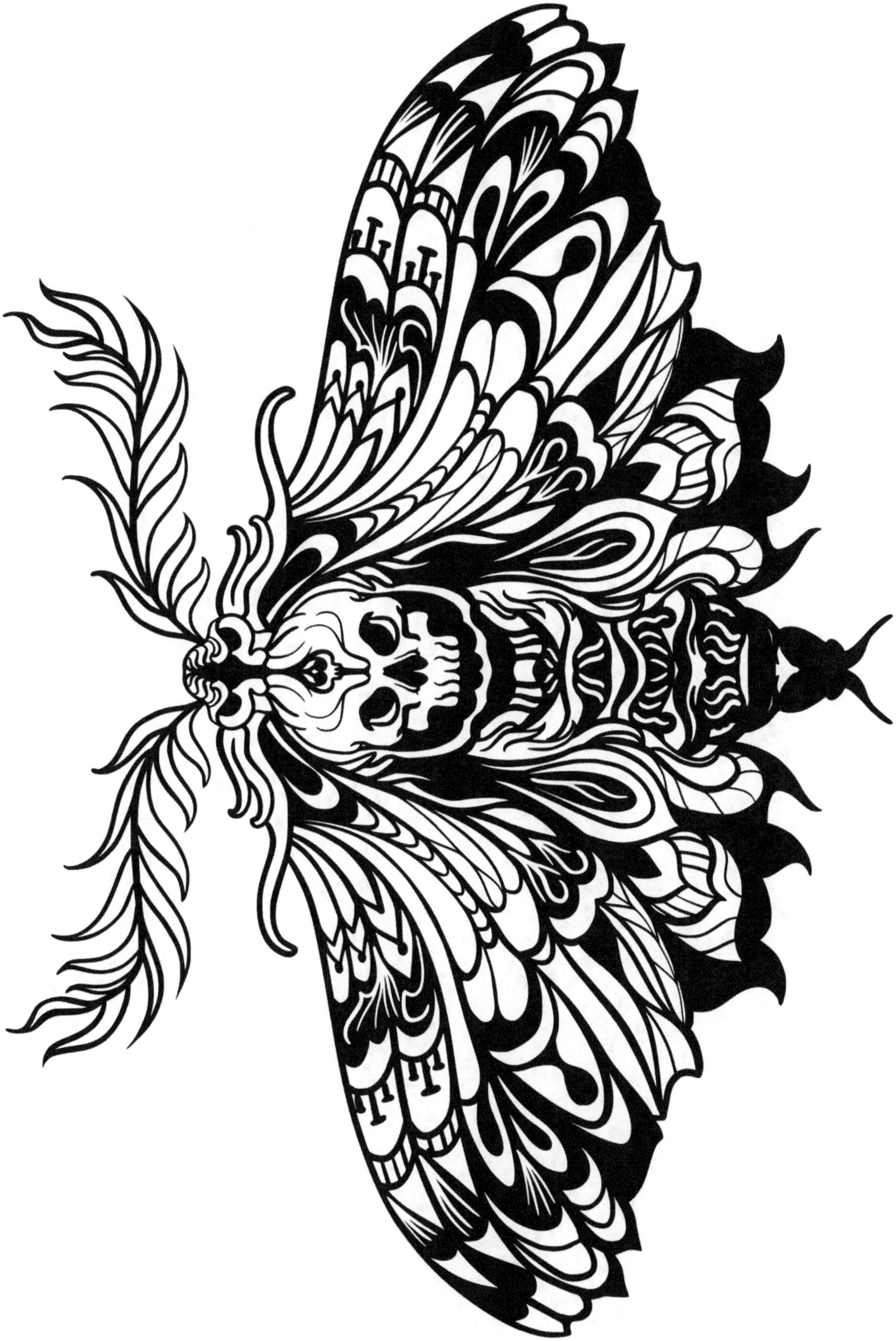

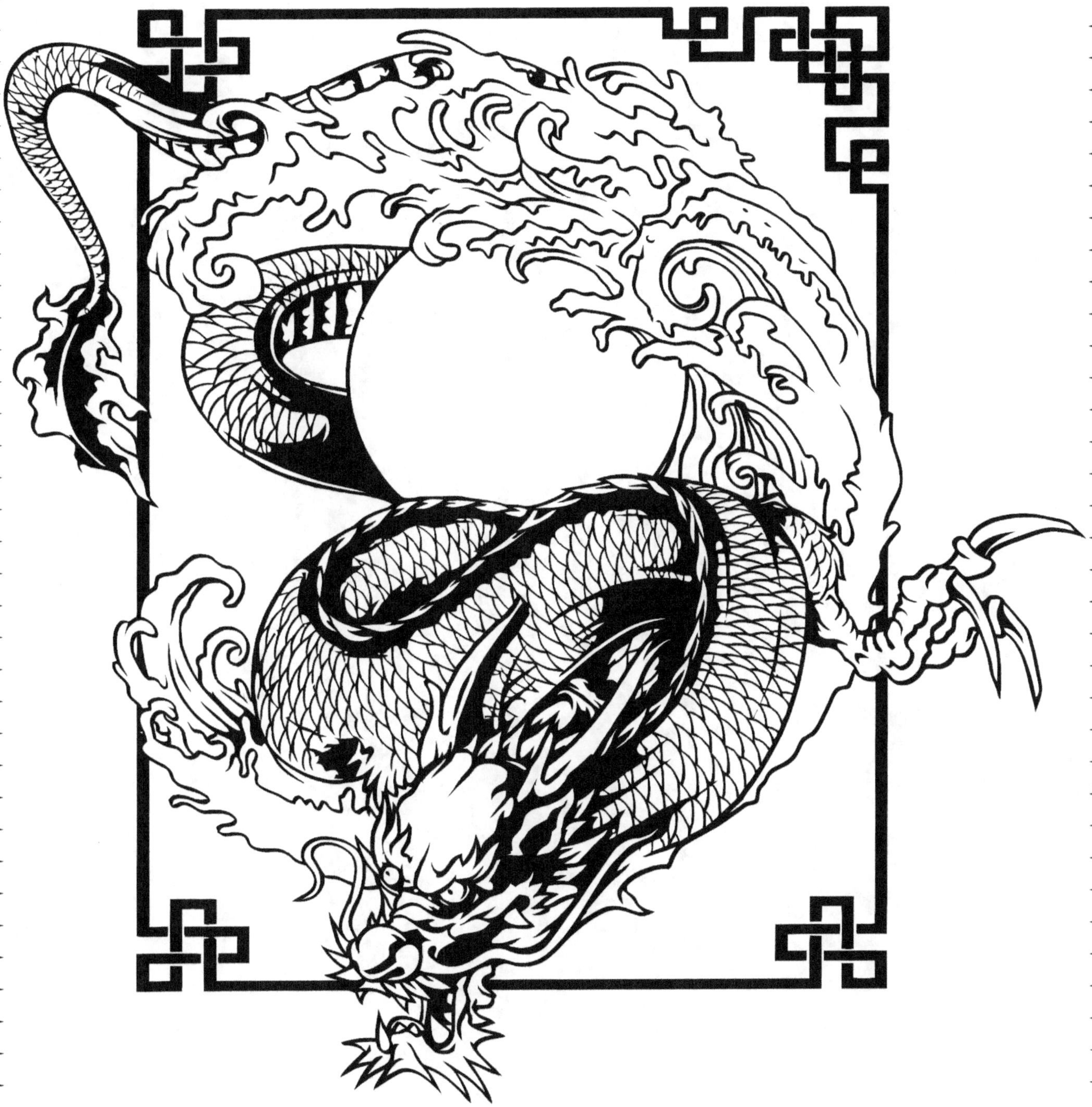

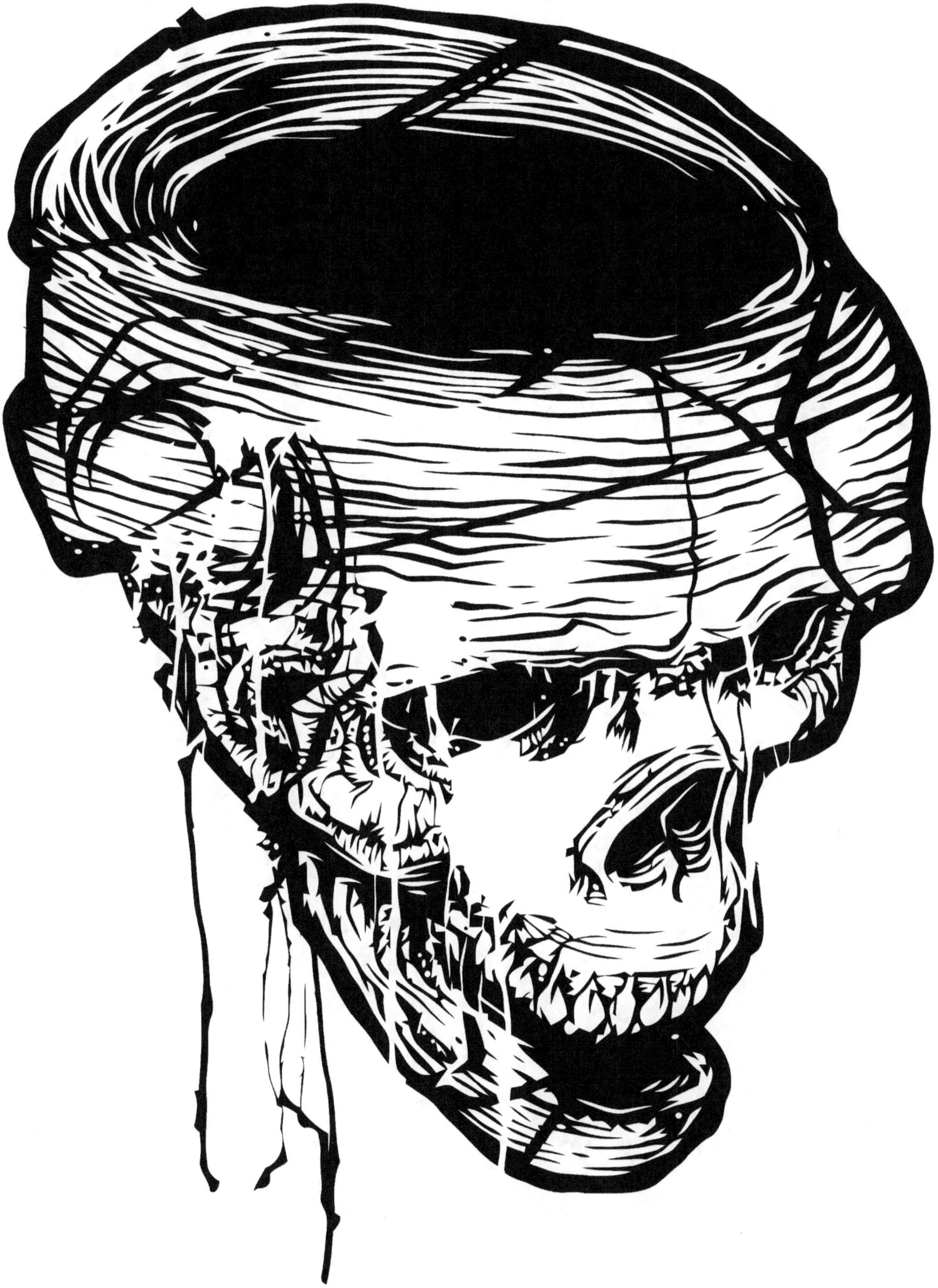

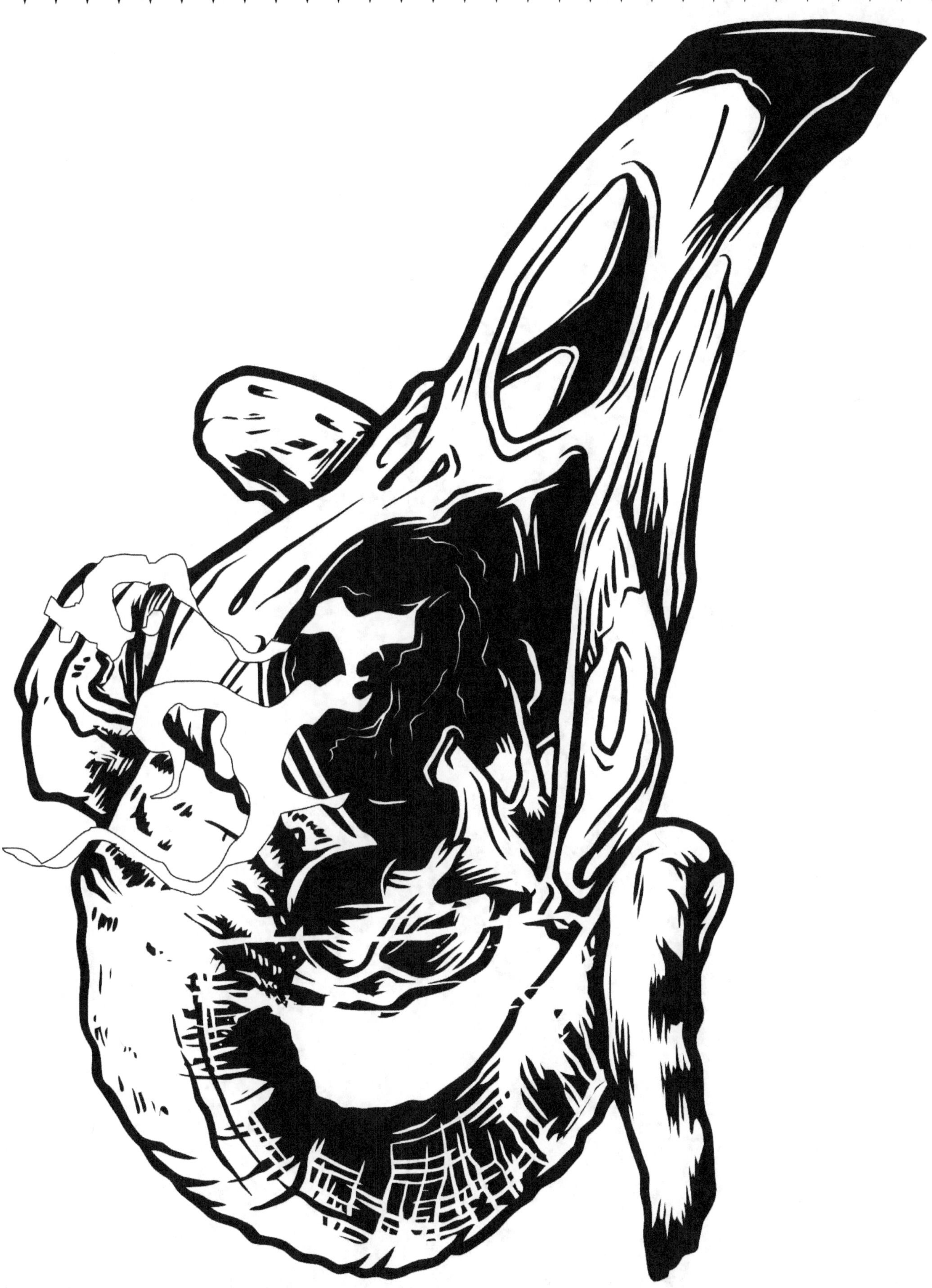

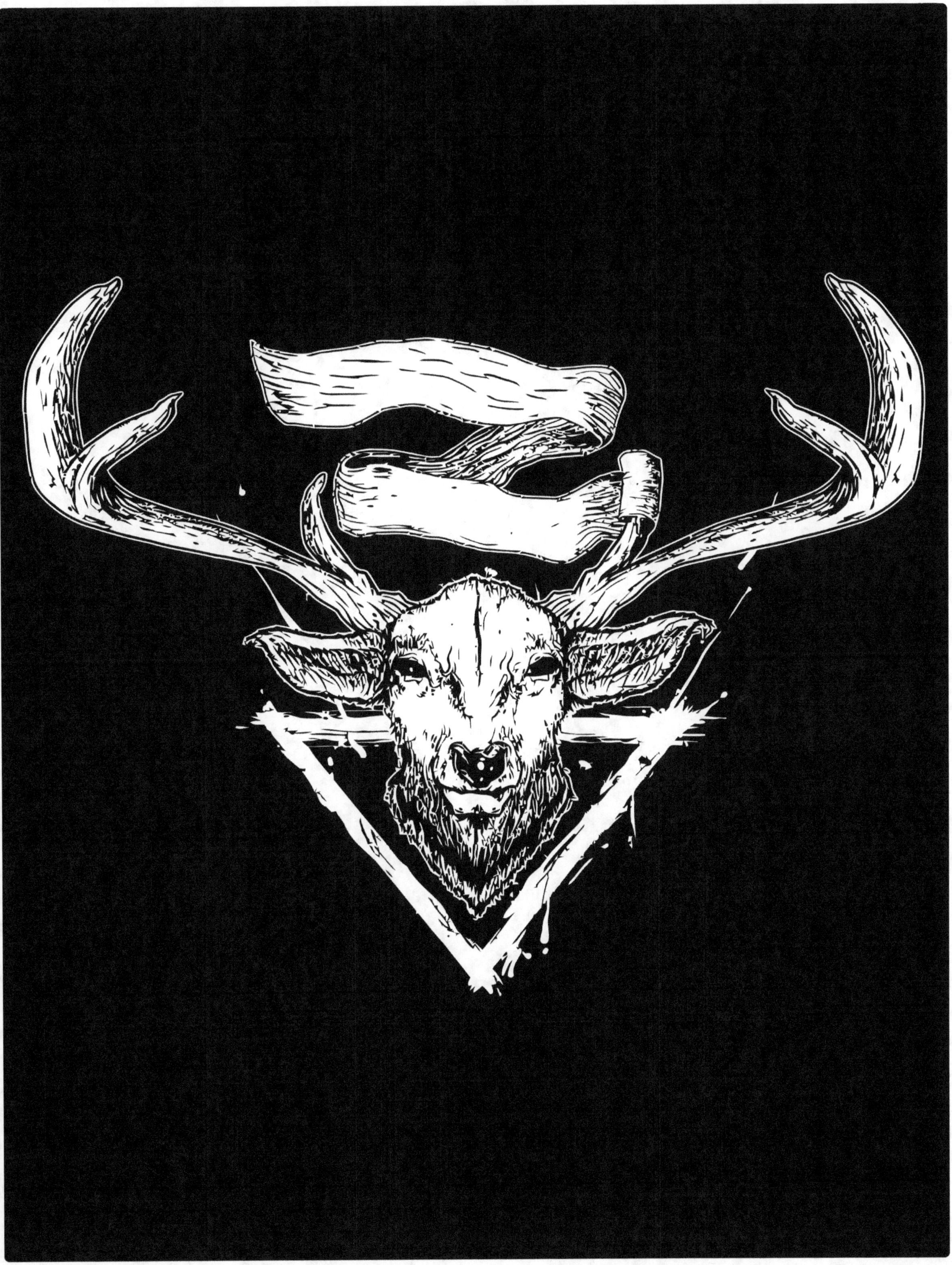

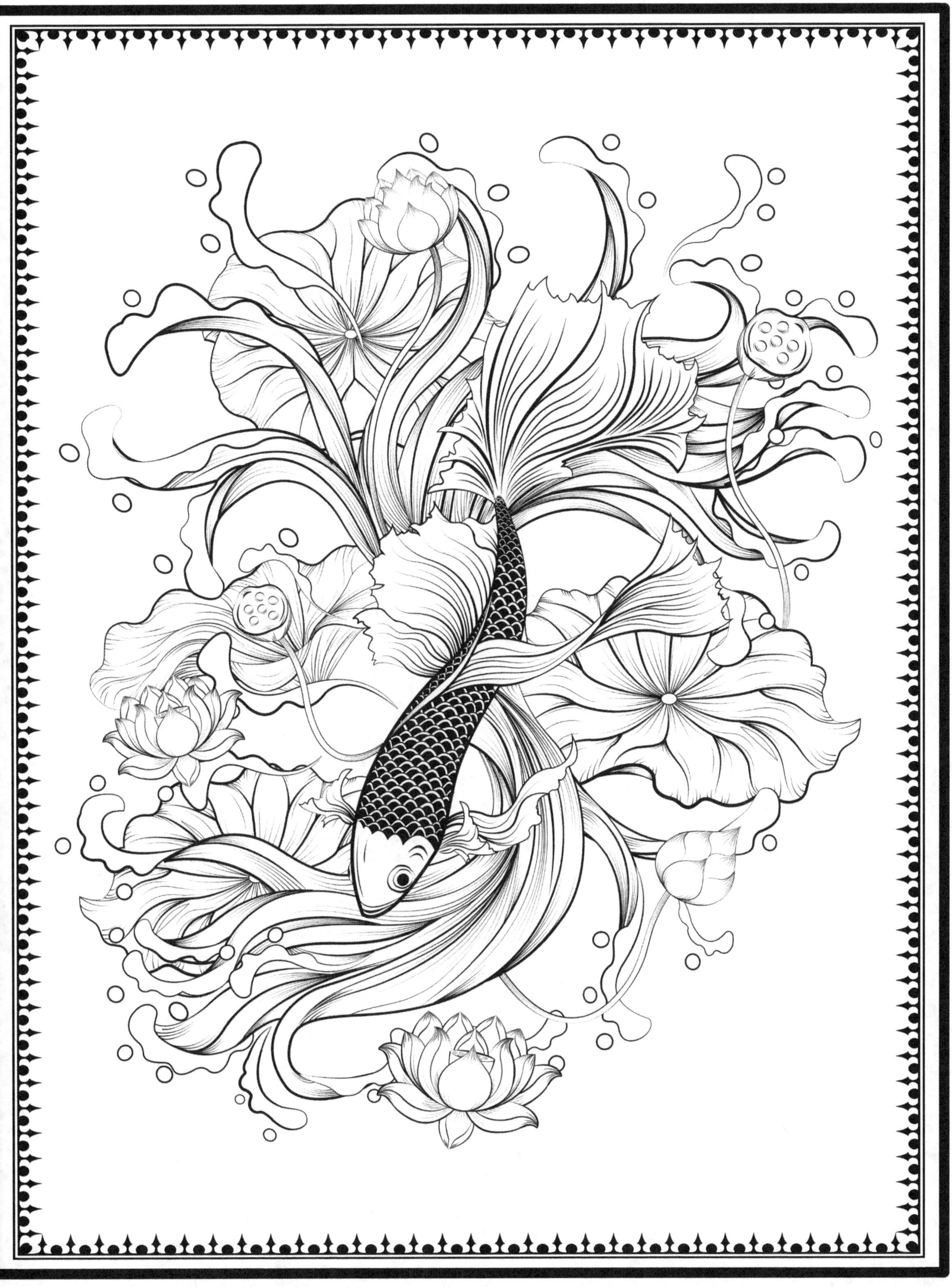

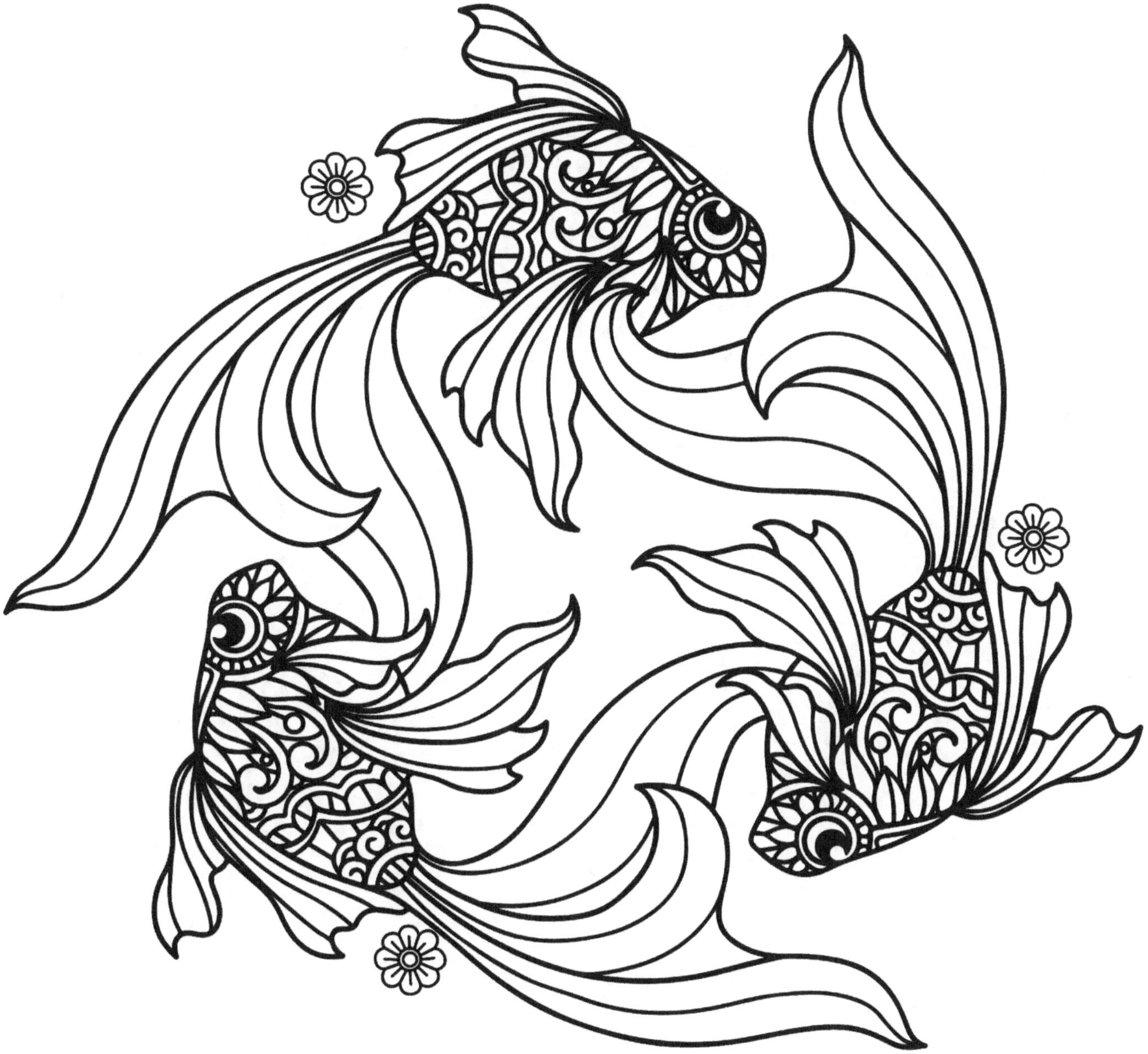

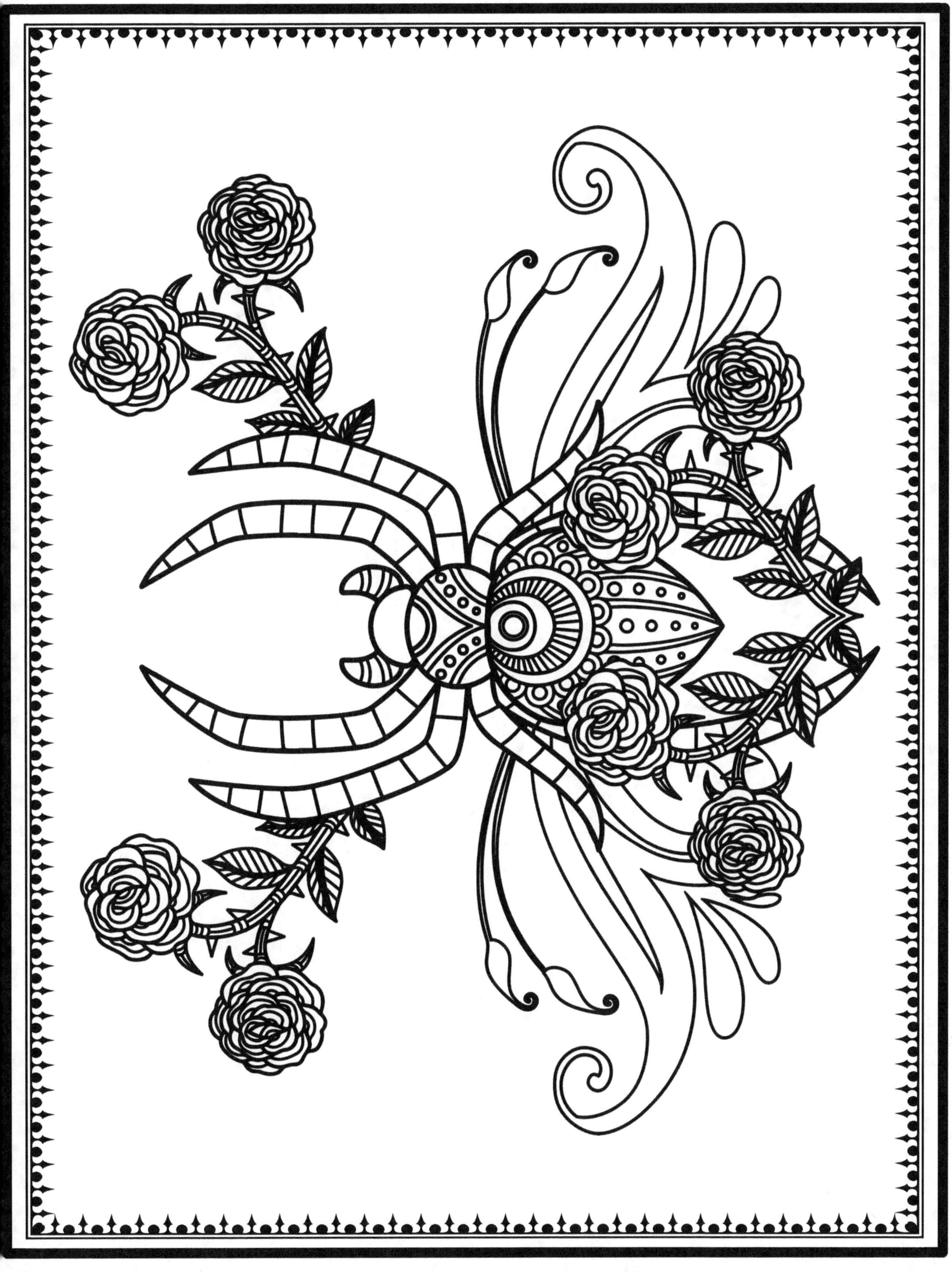

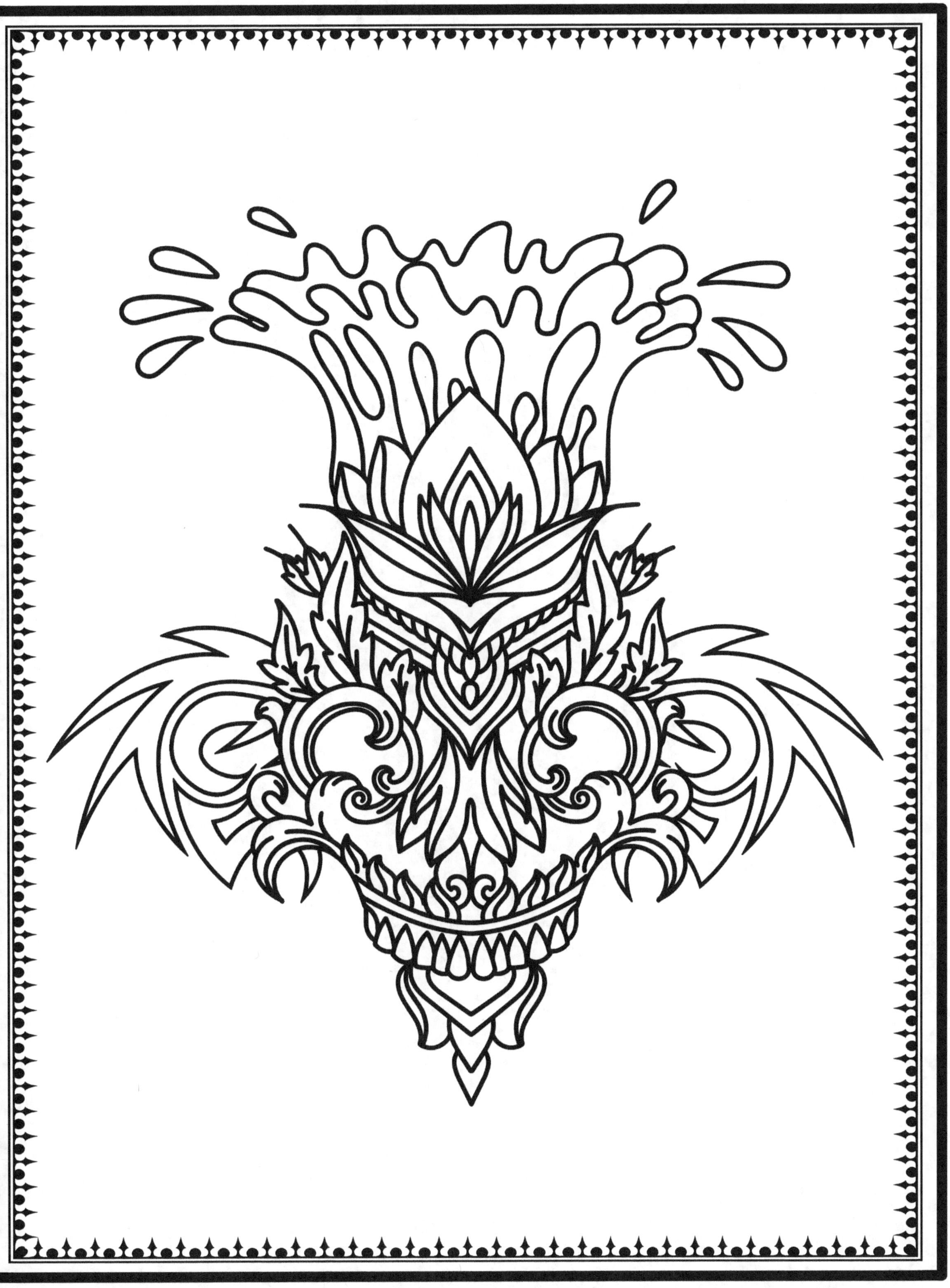

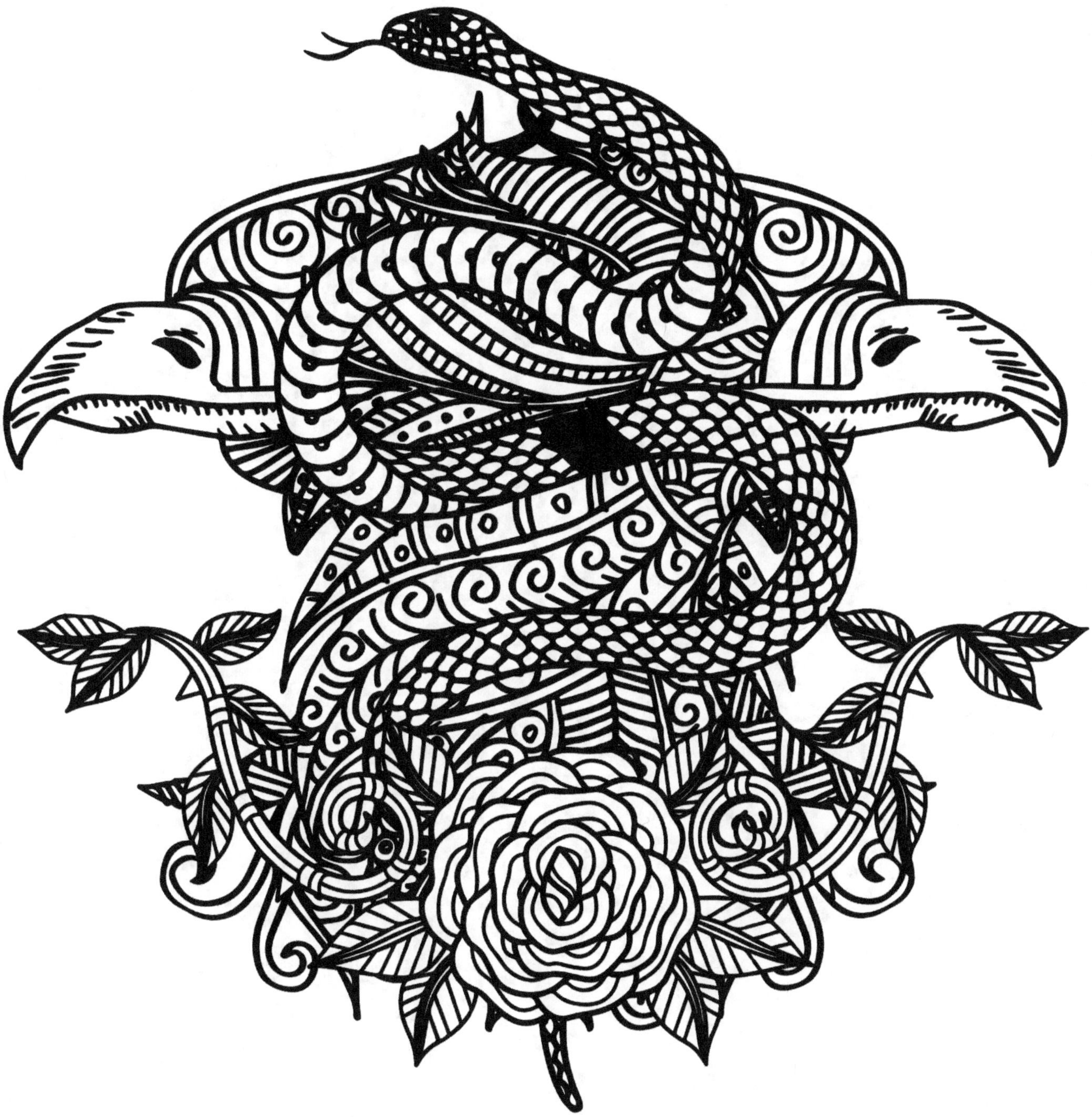

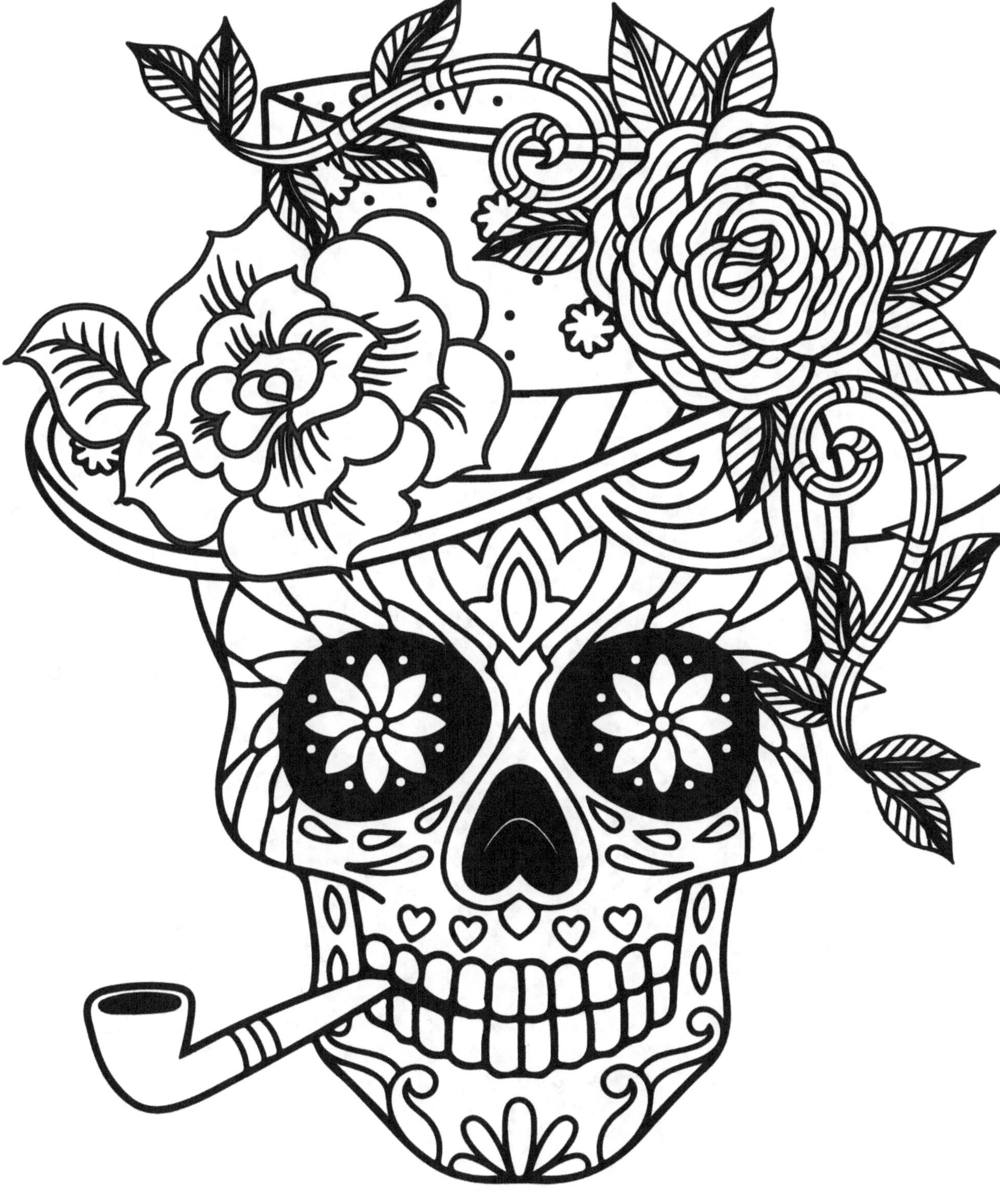

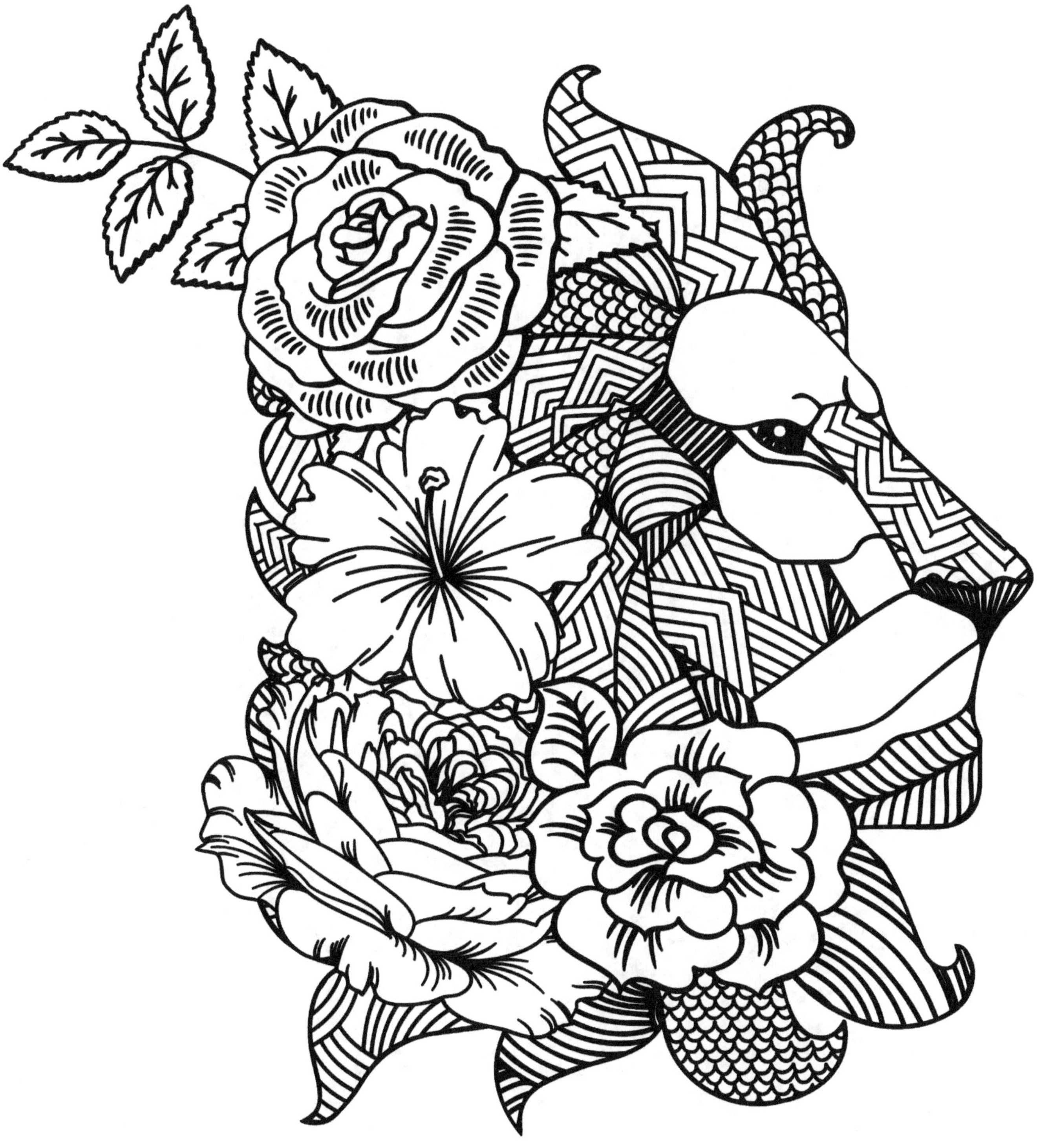

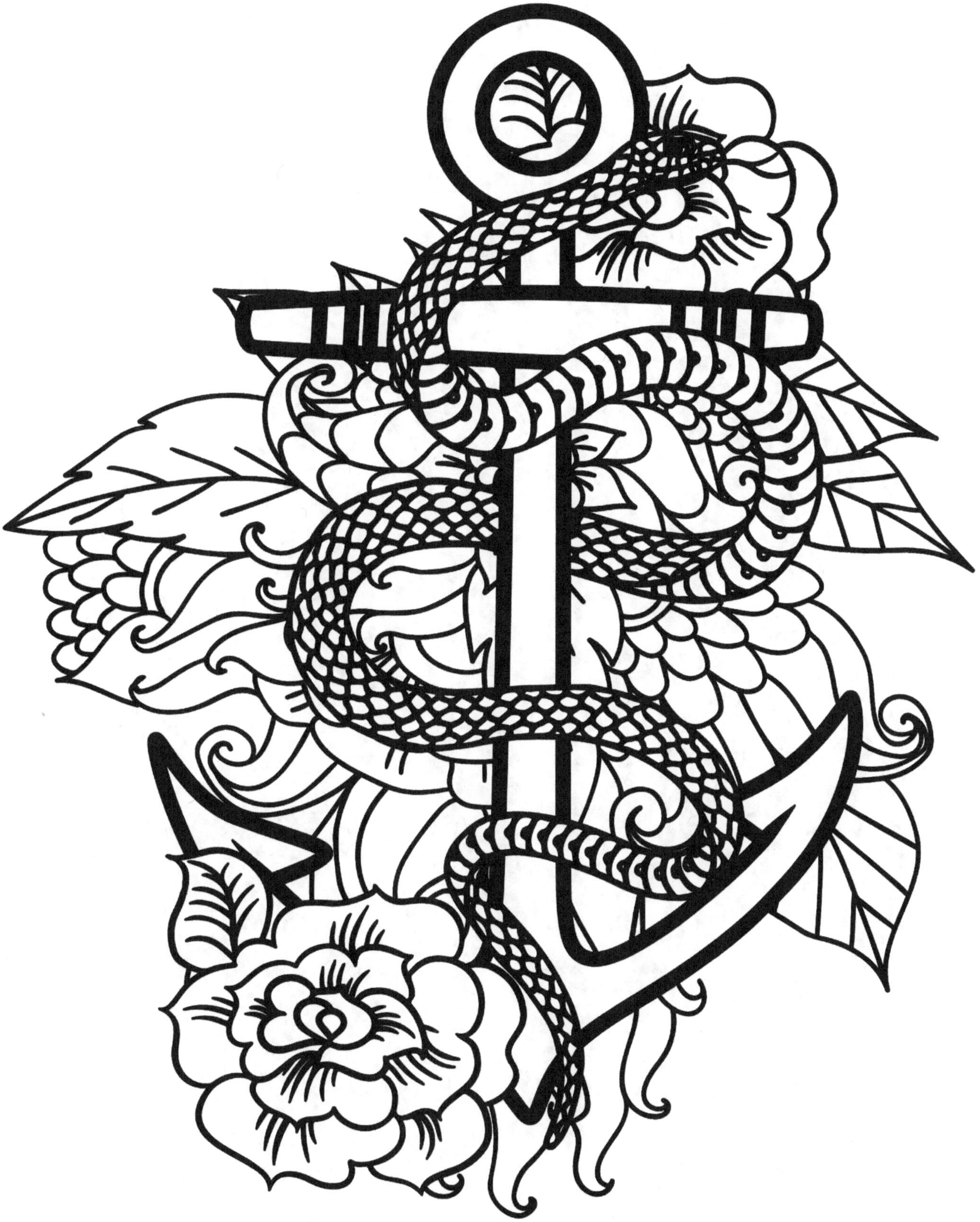

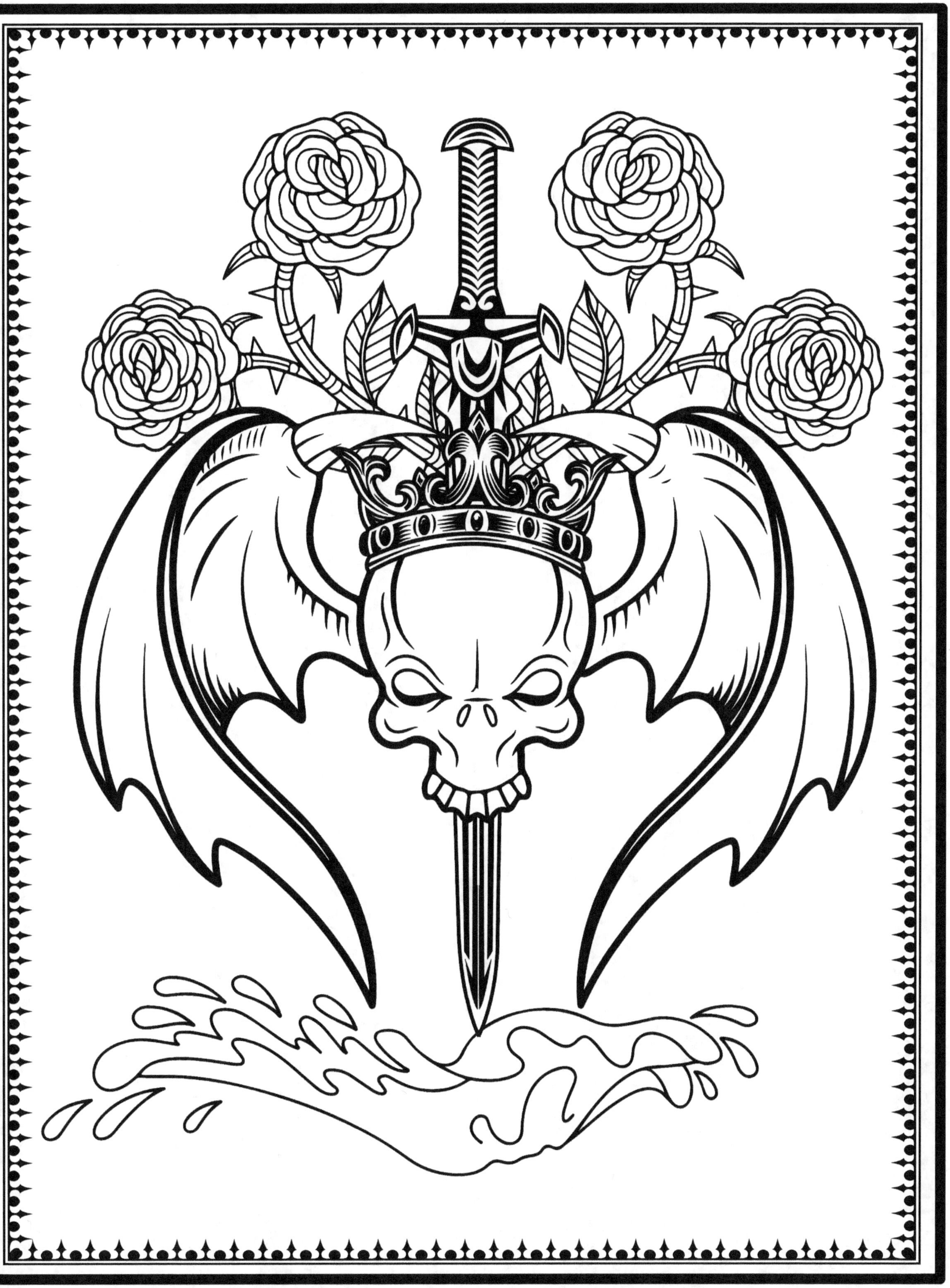

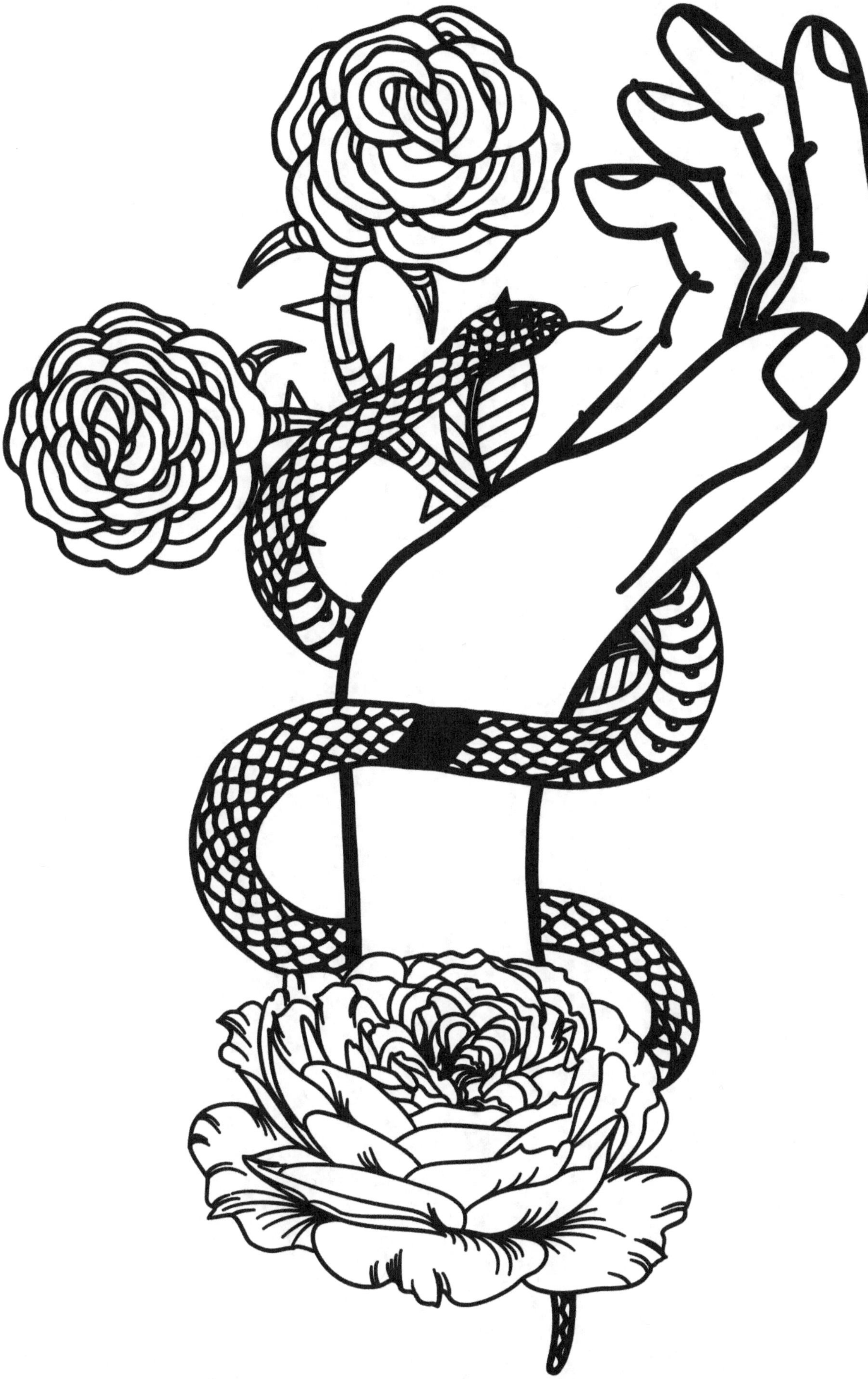

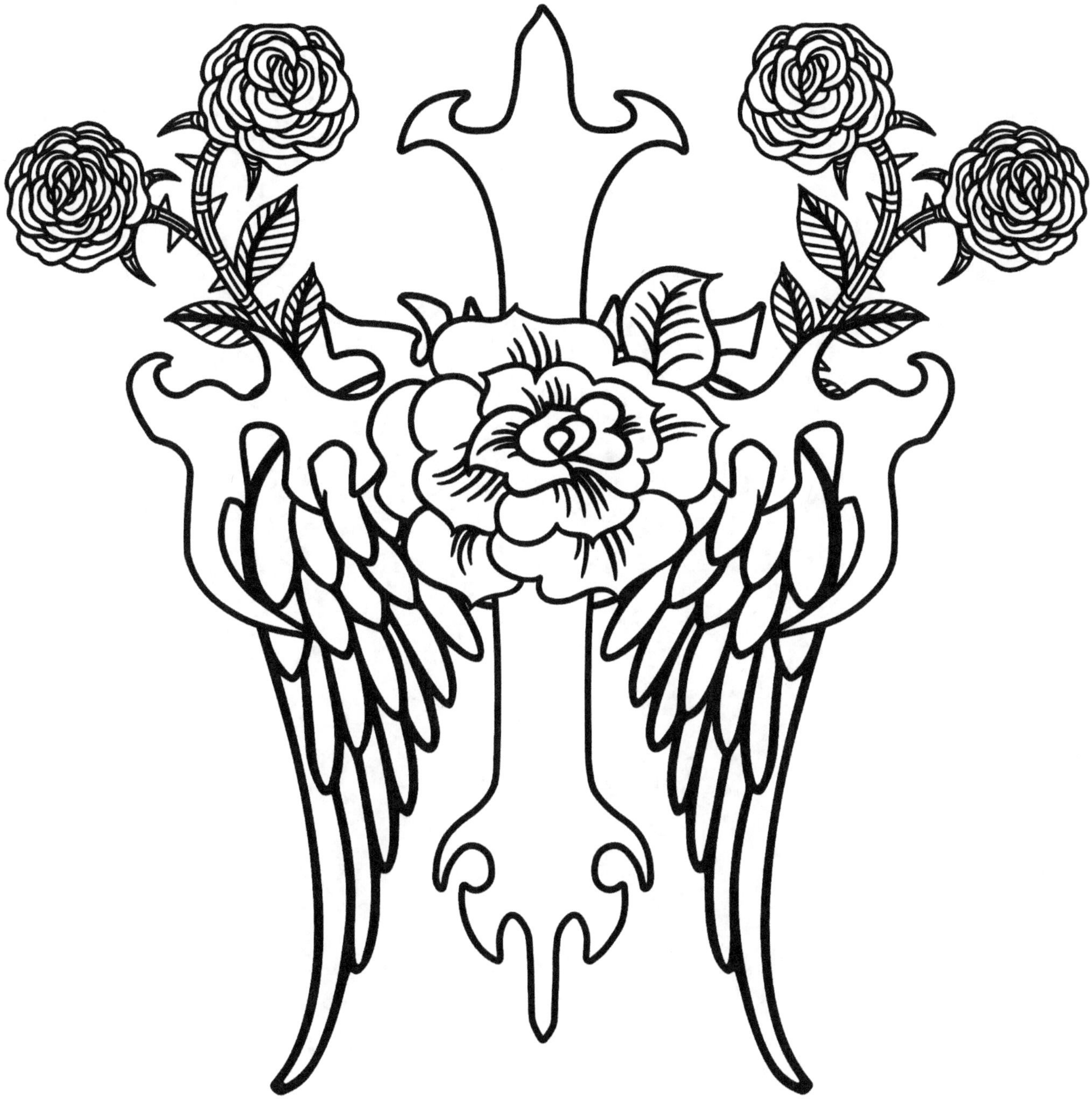

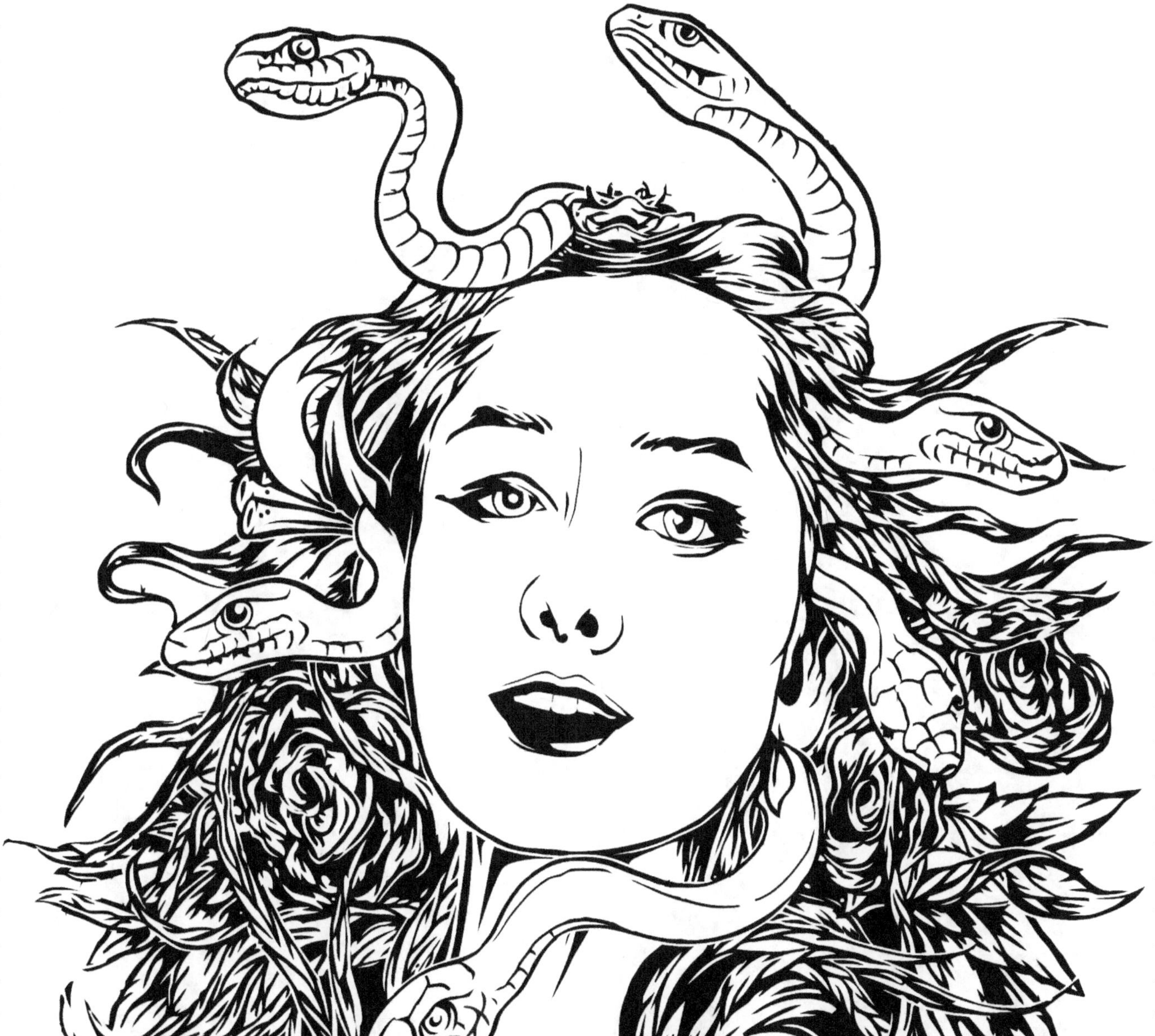

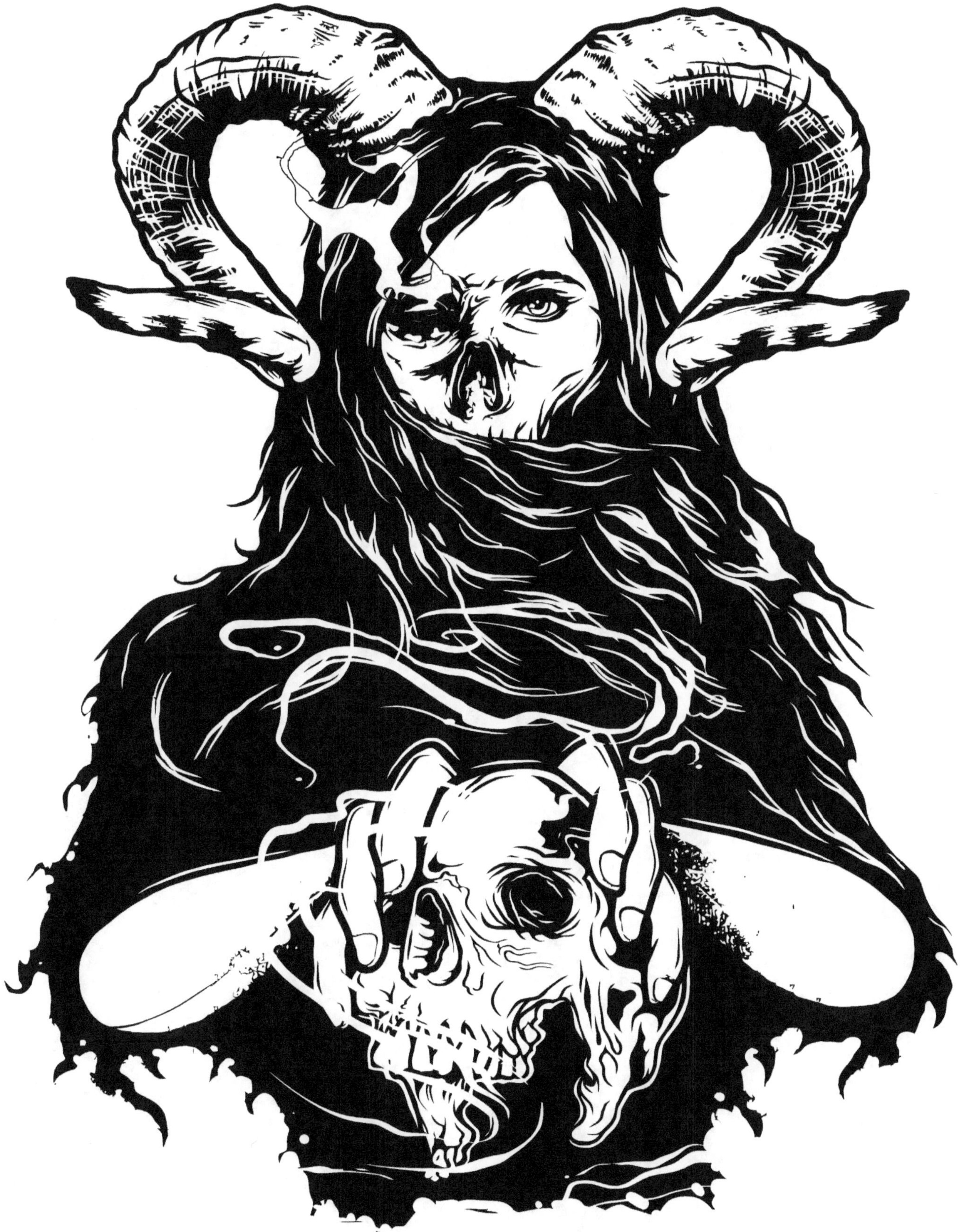

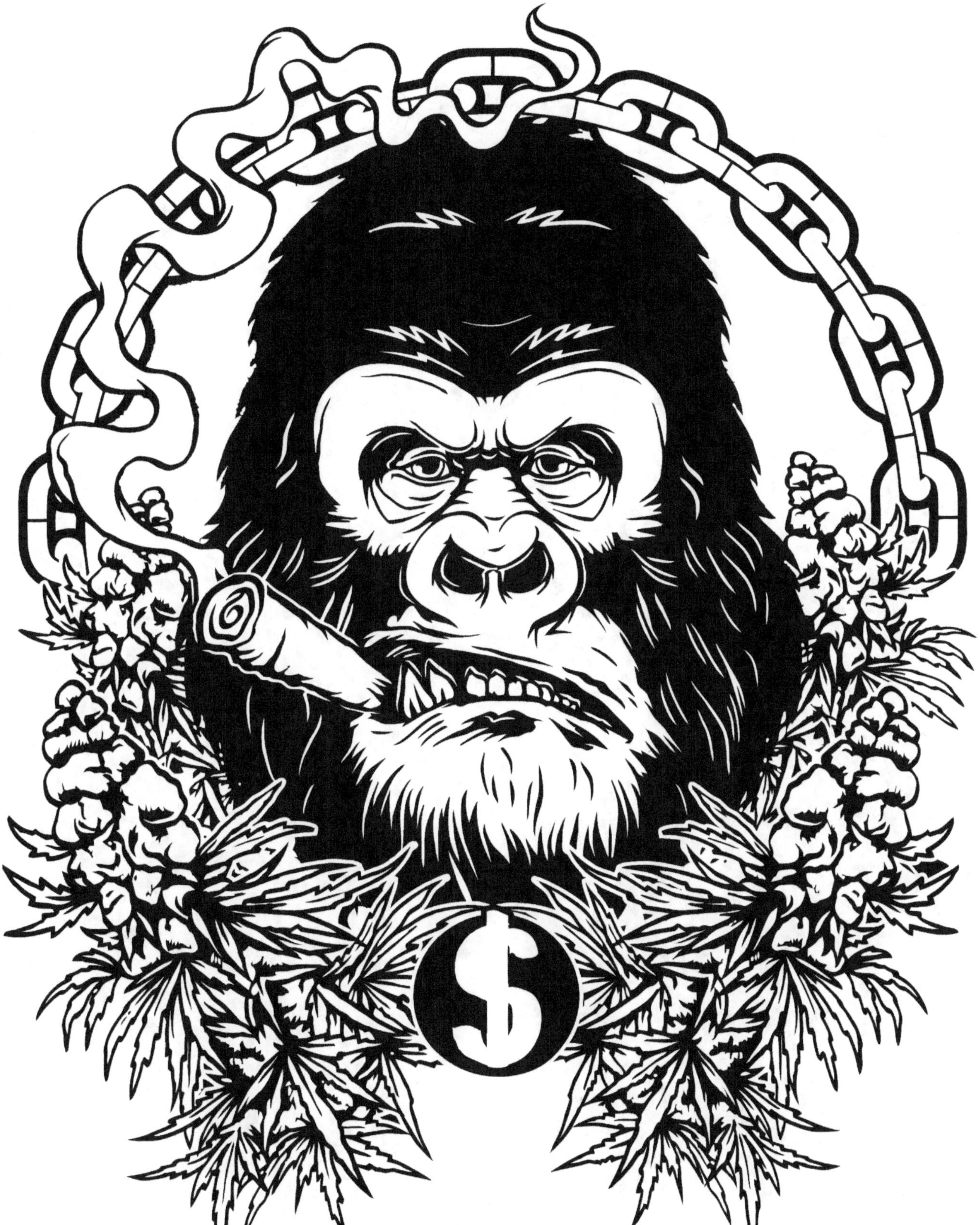

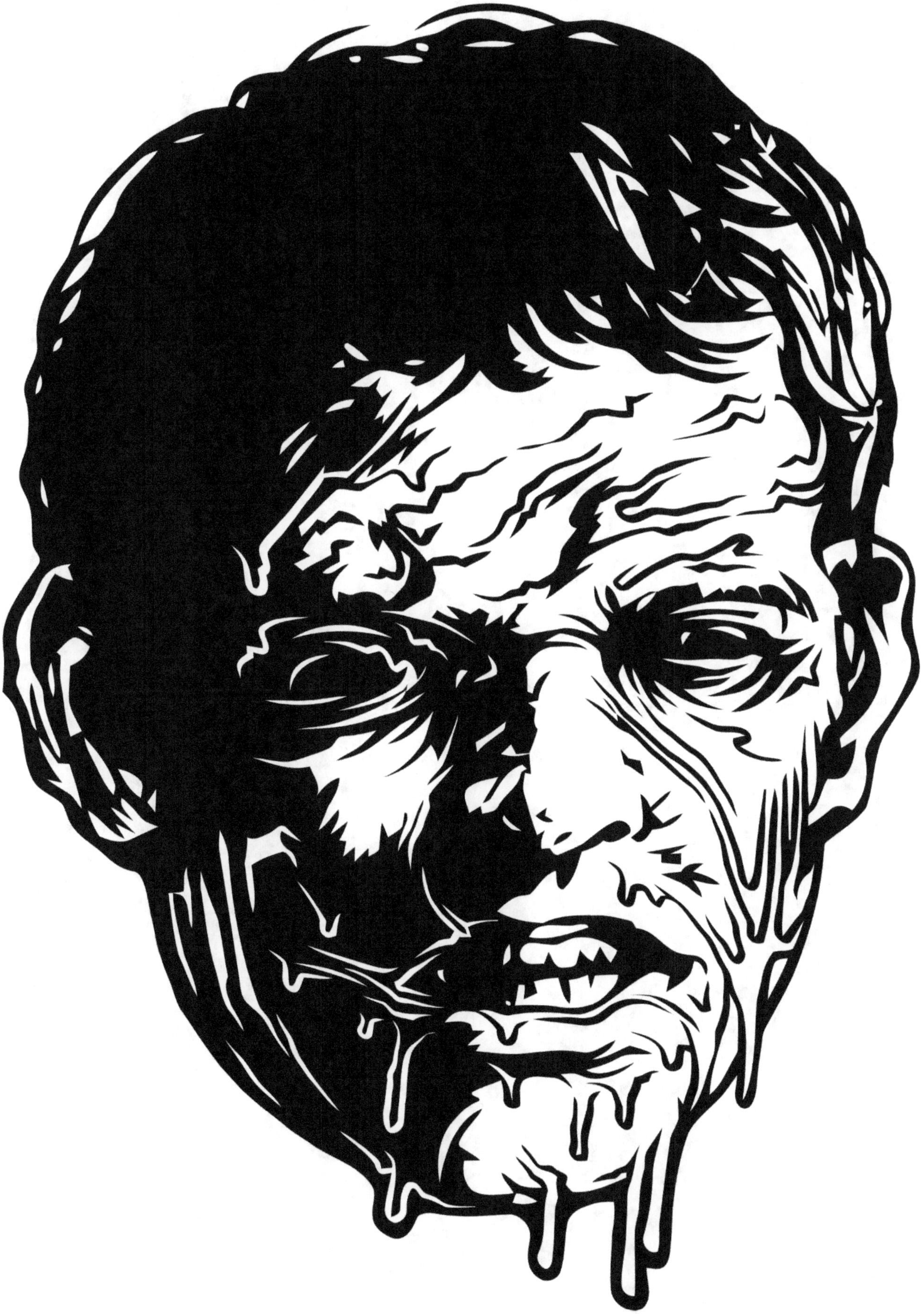

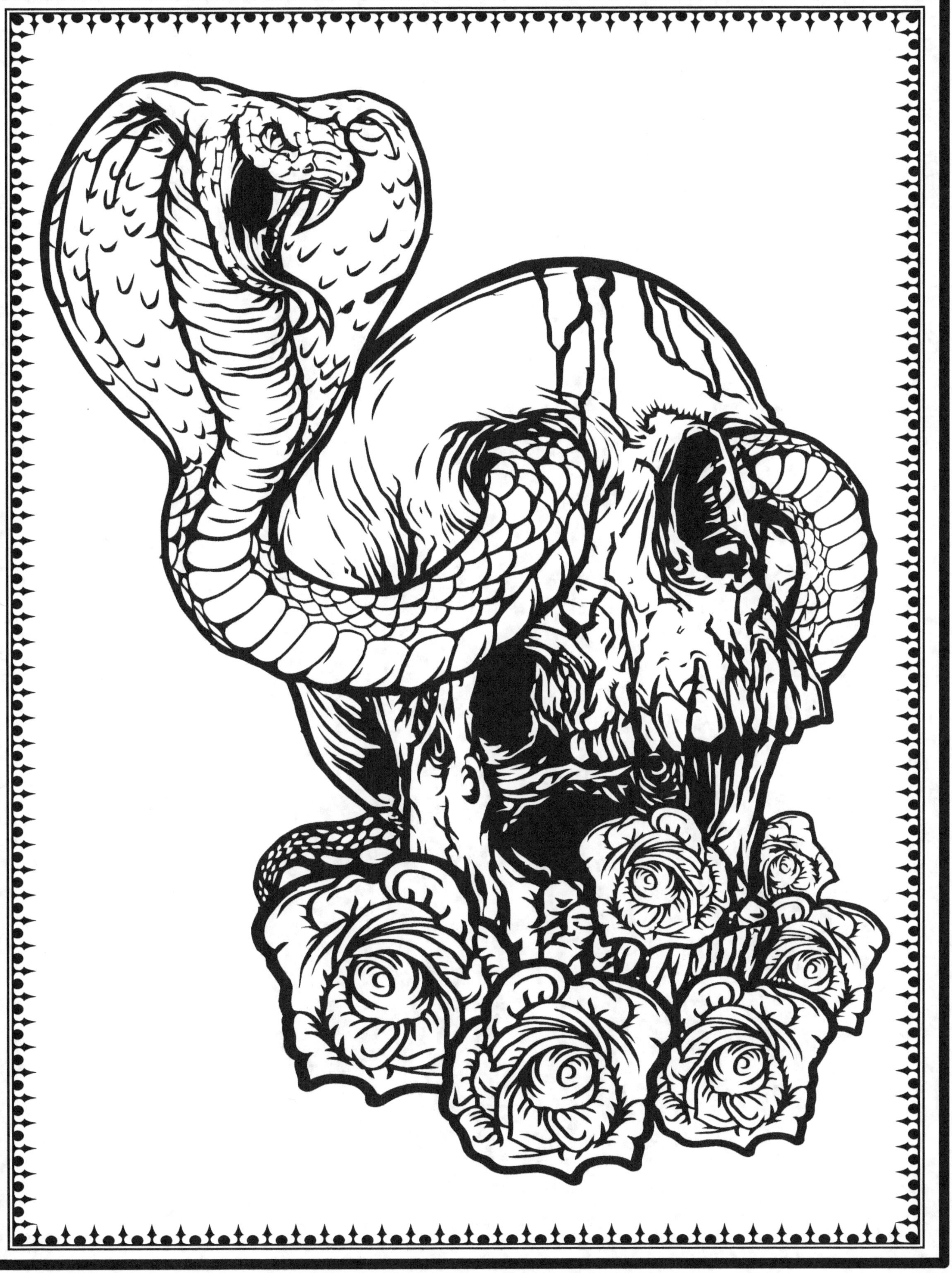

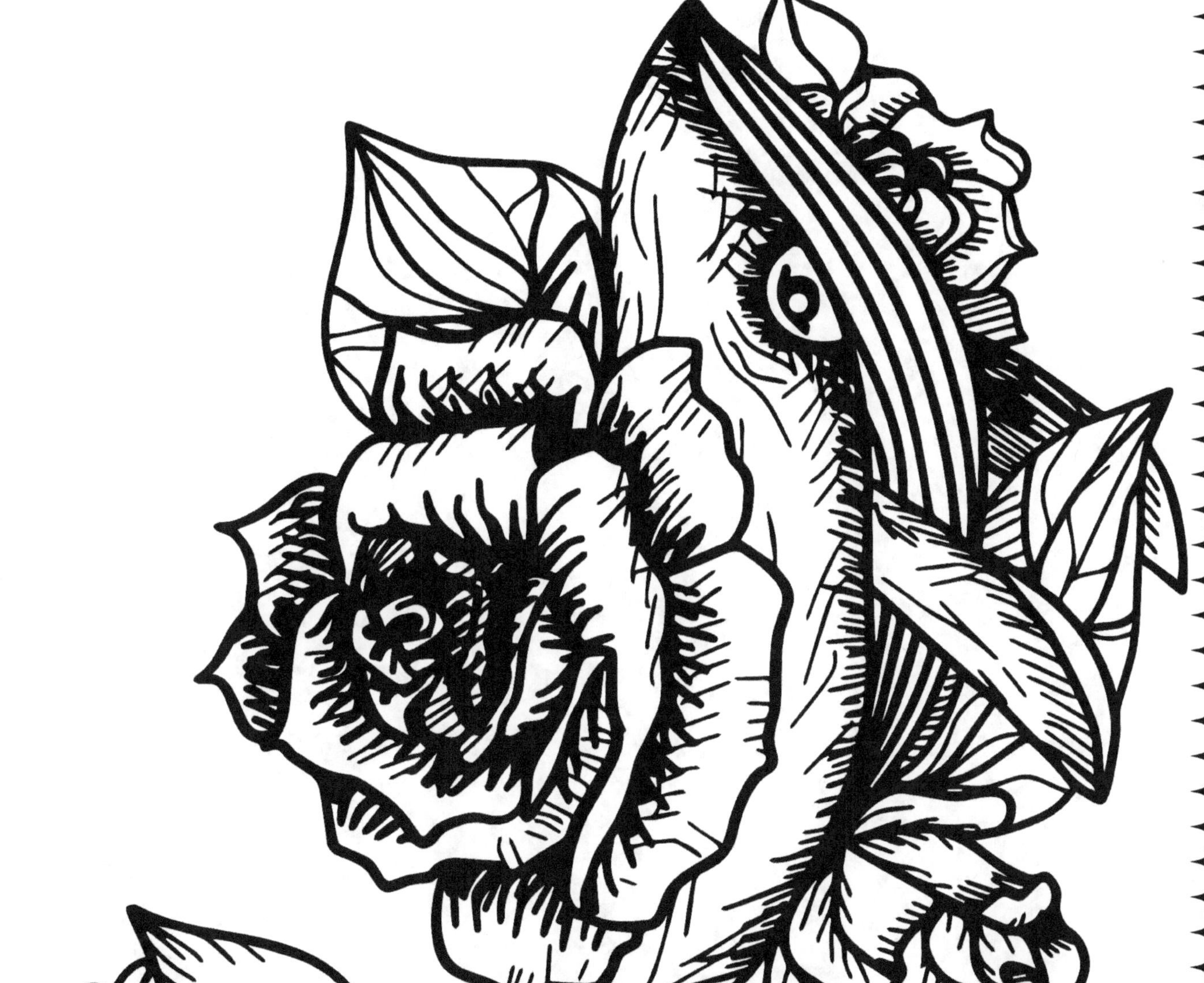

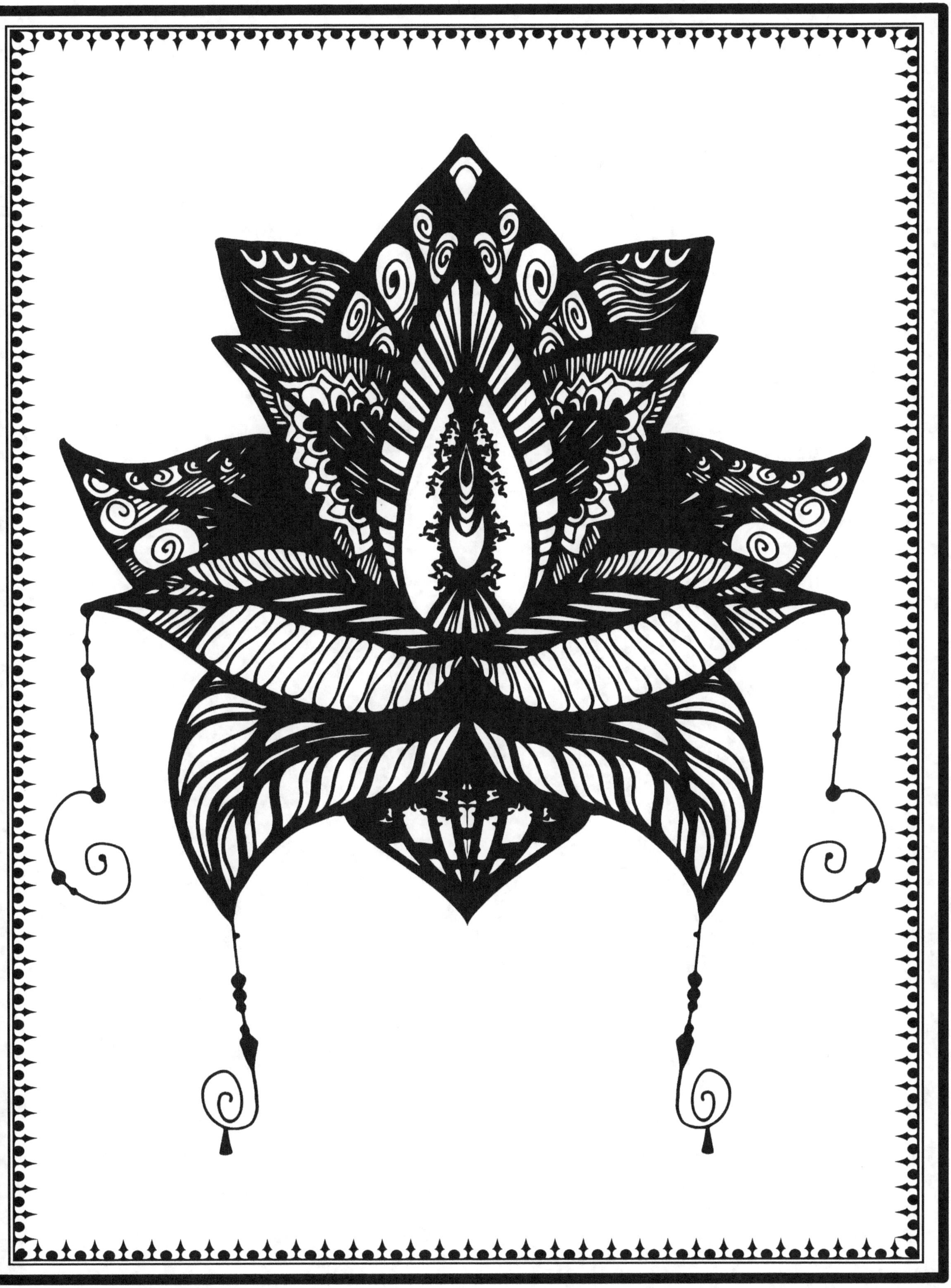

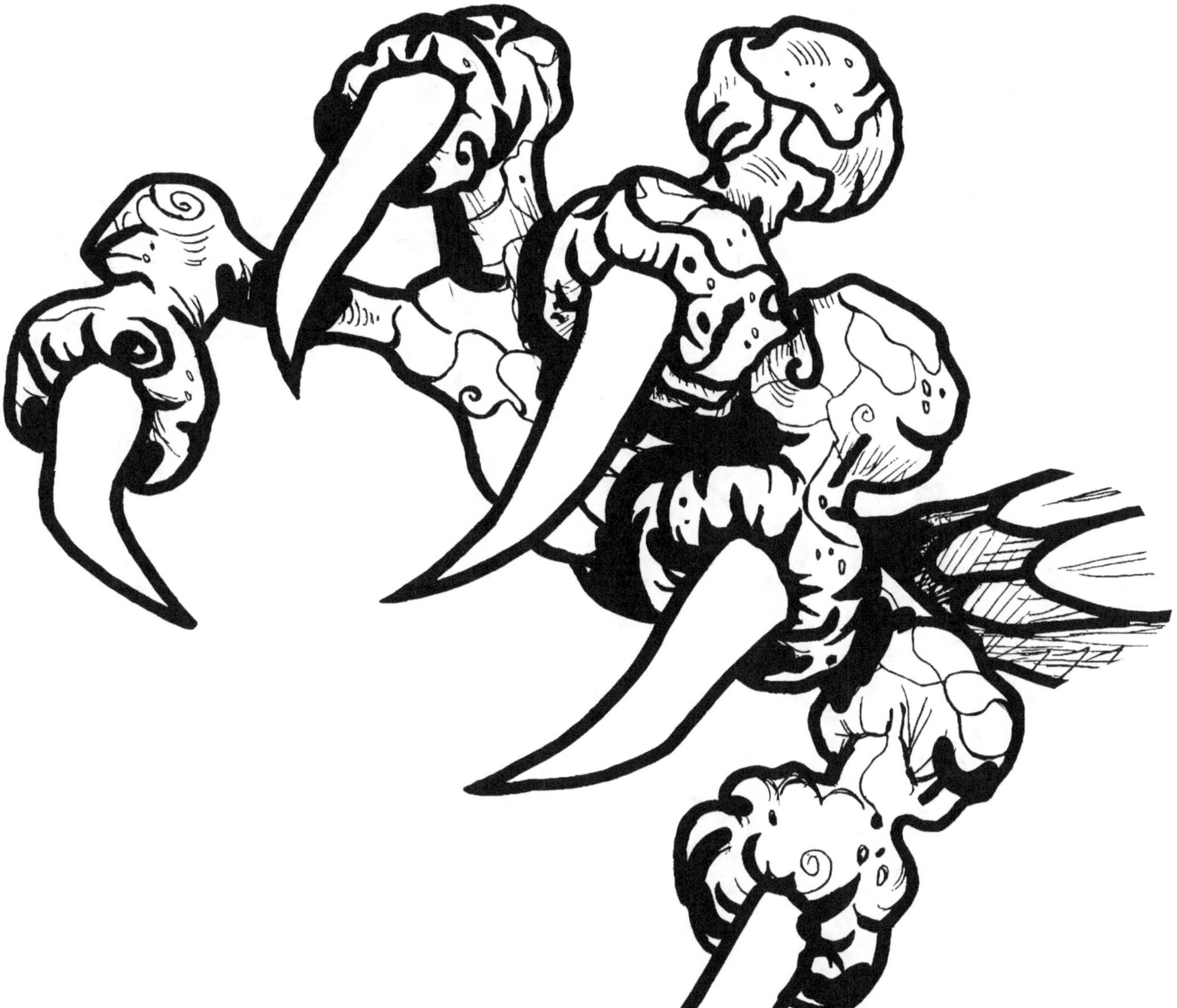

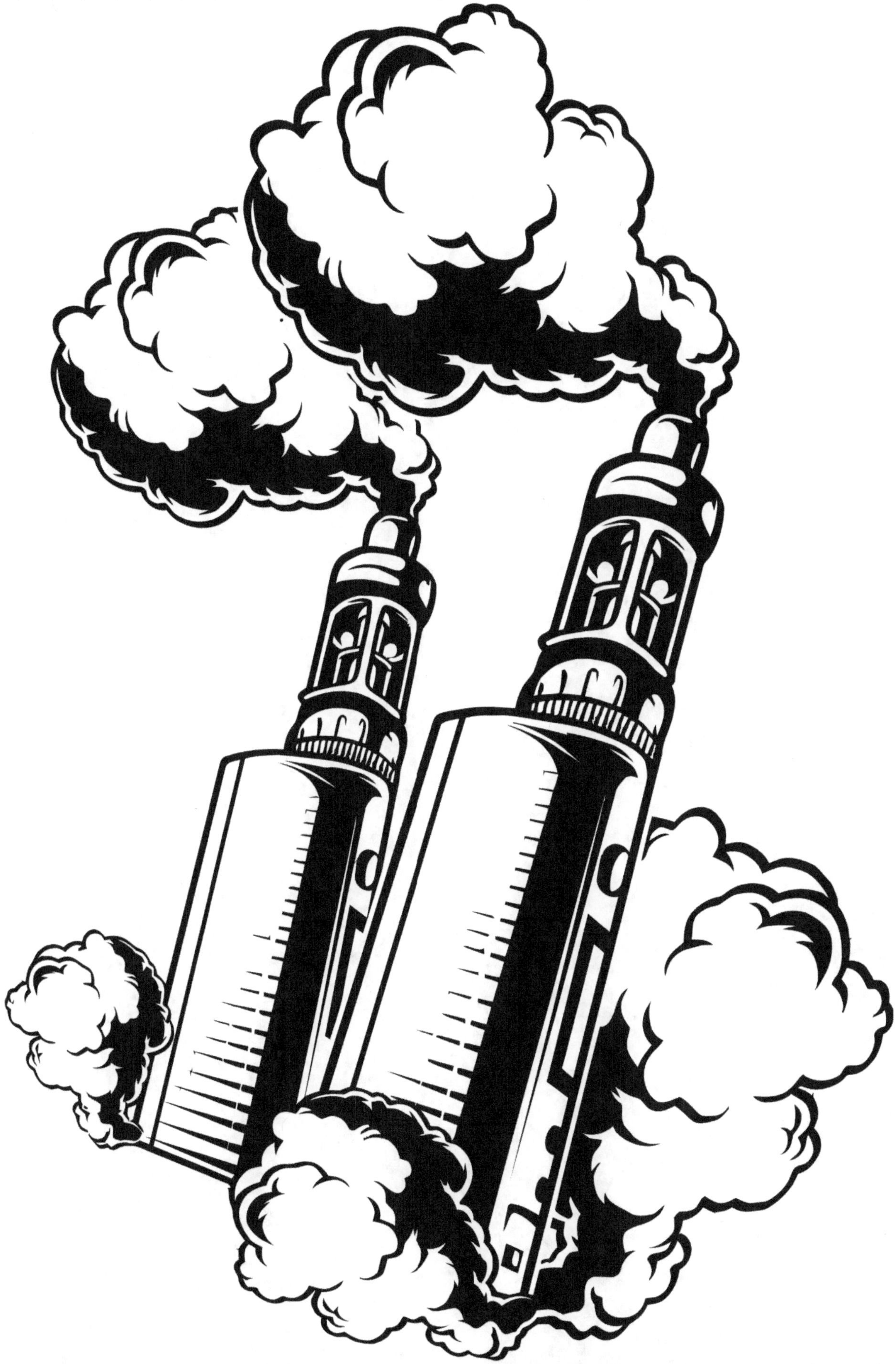

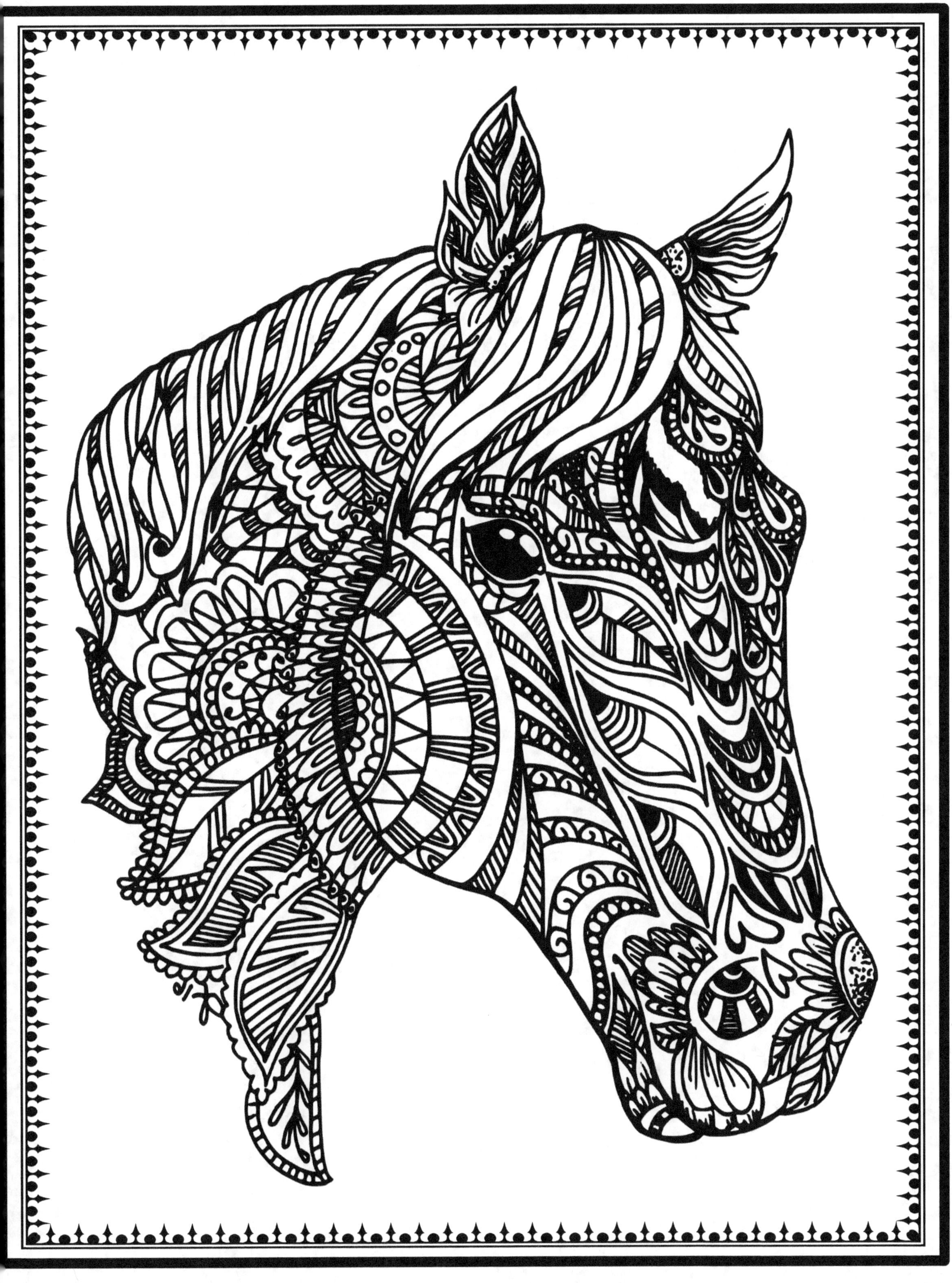

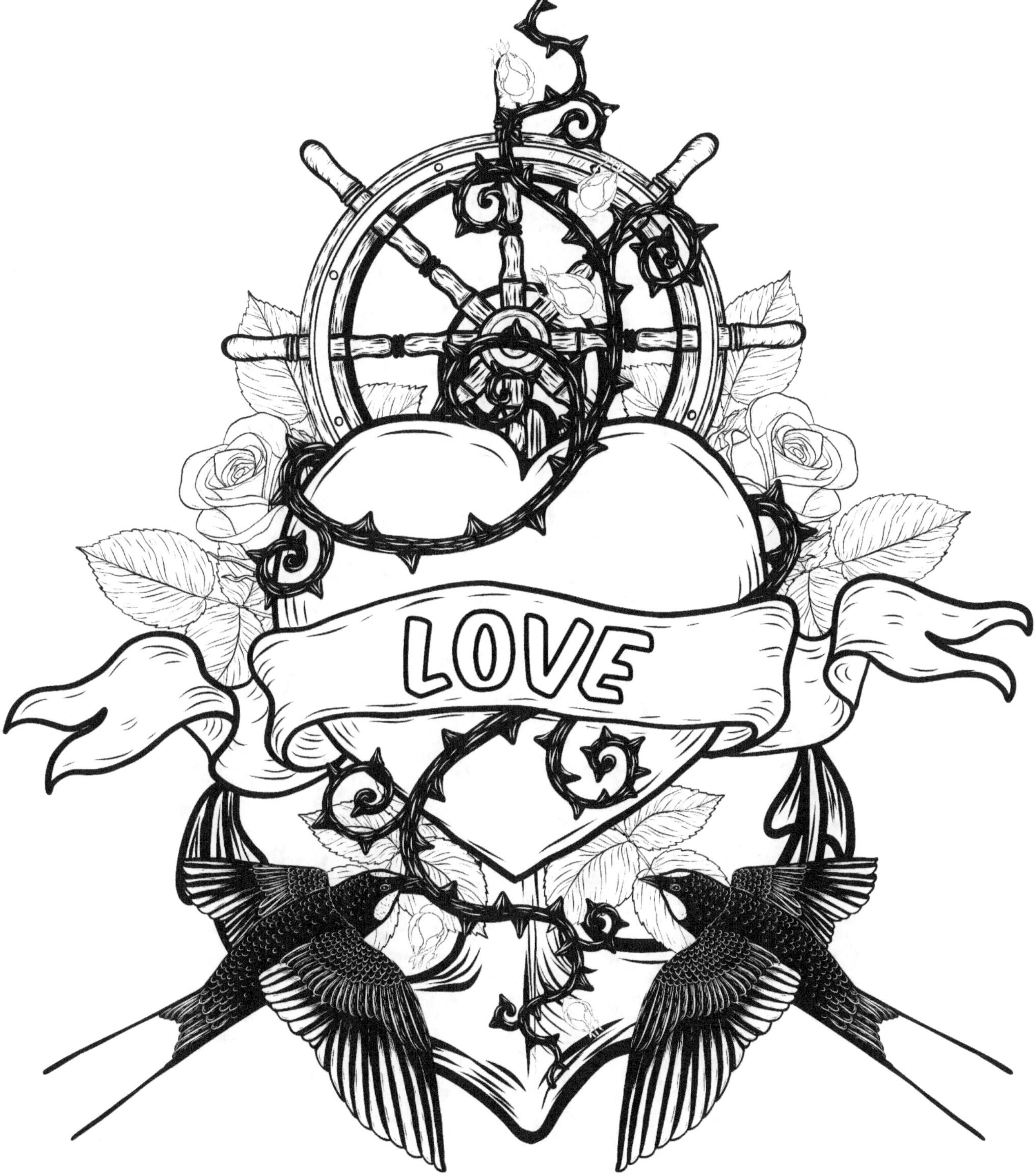
LOVE

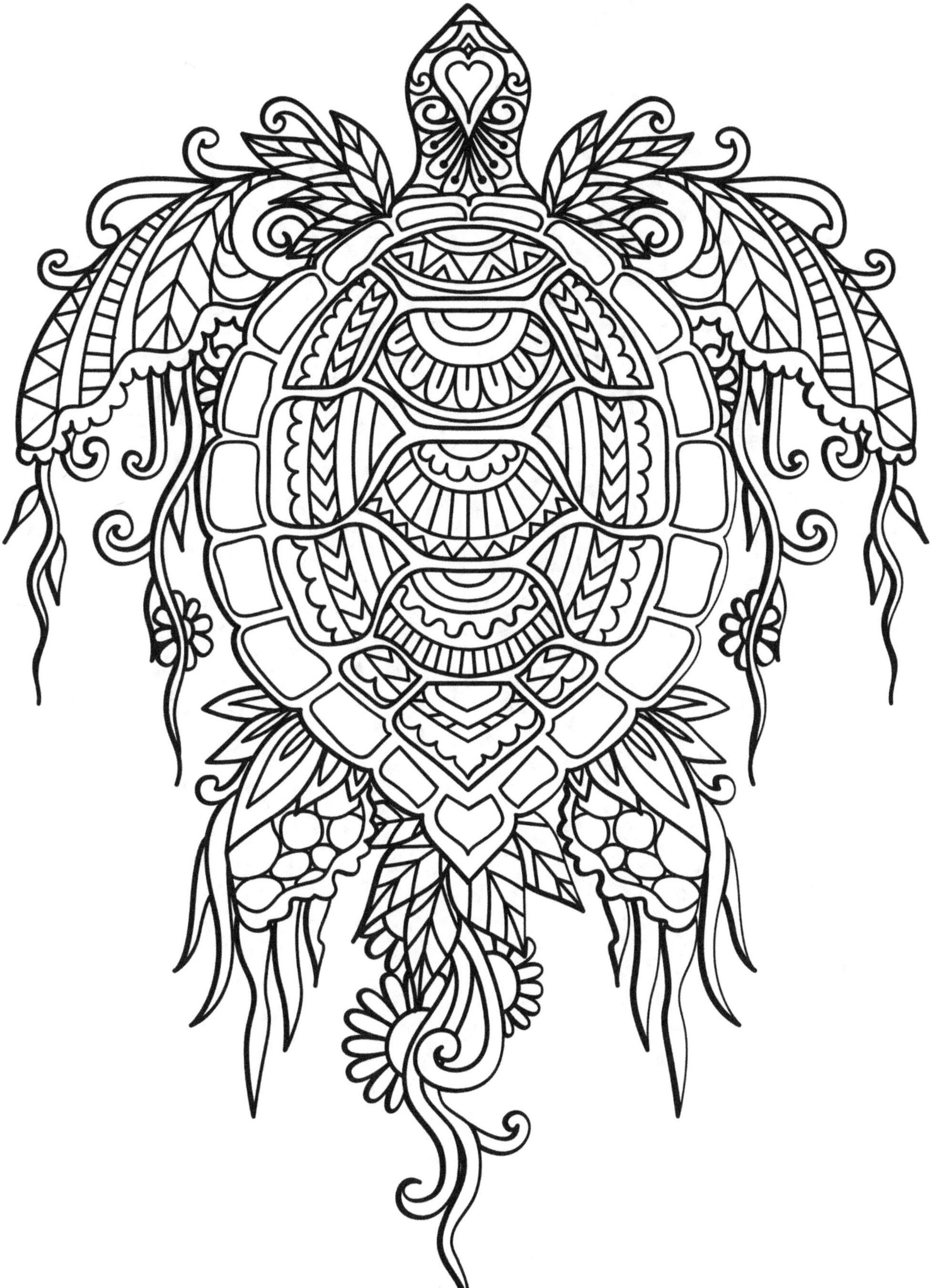

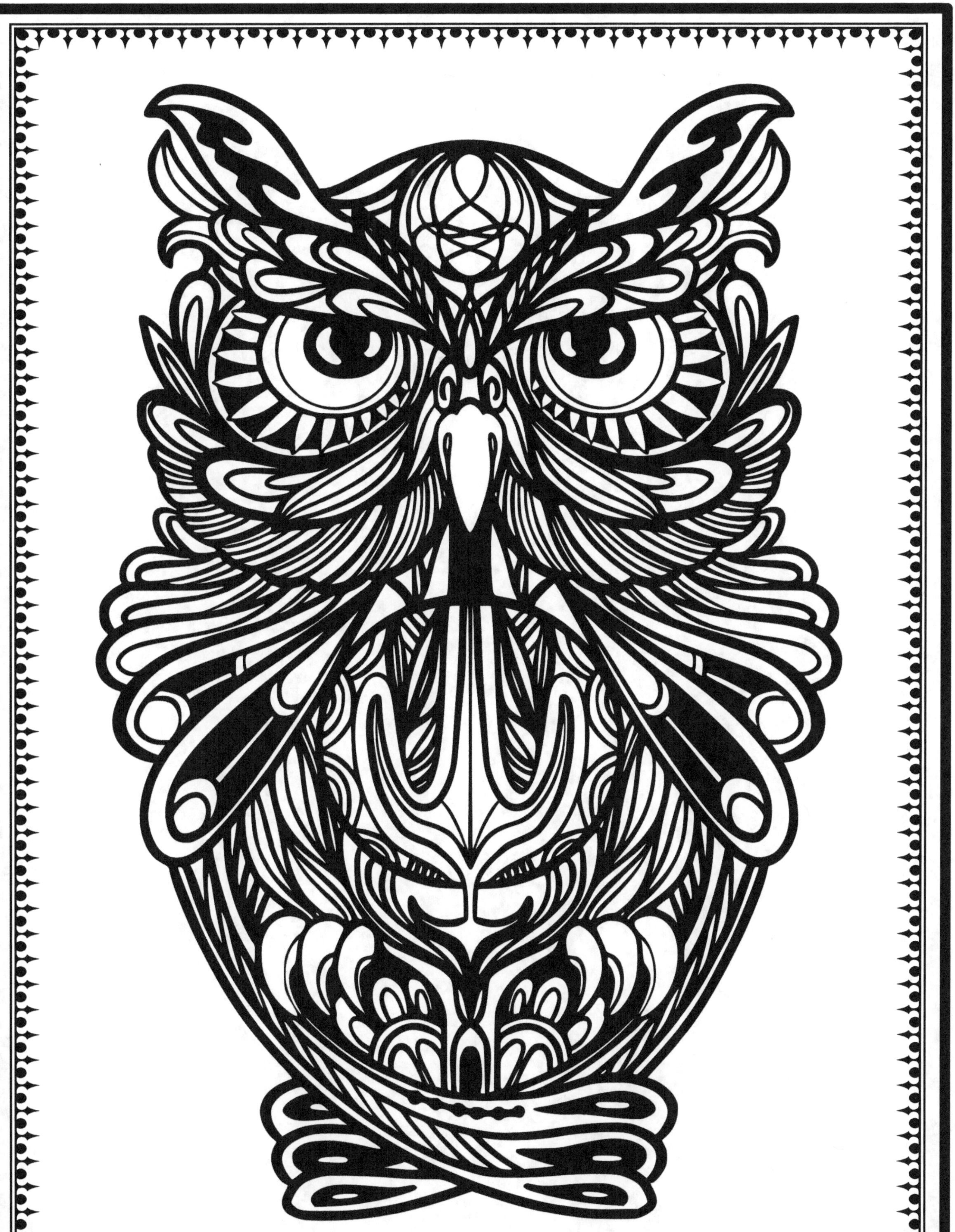

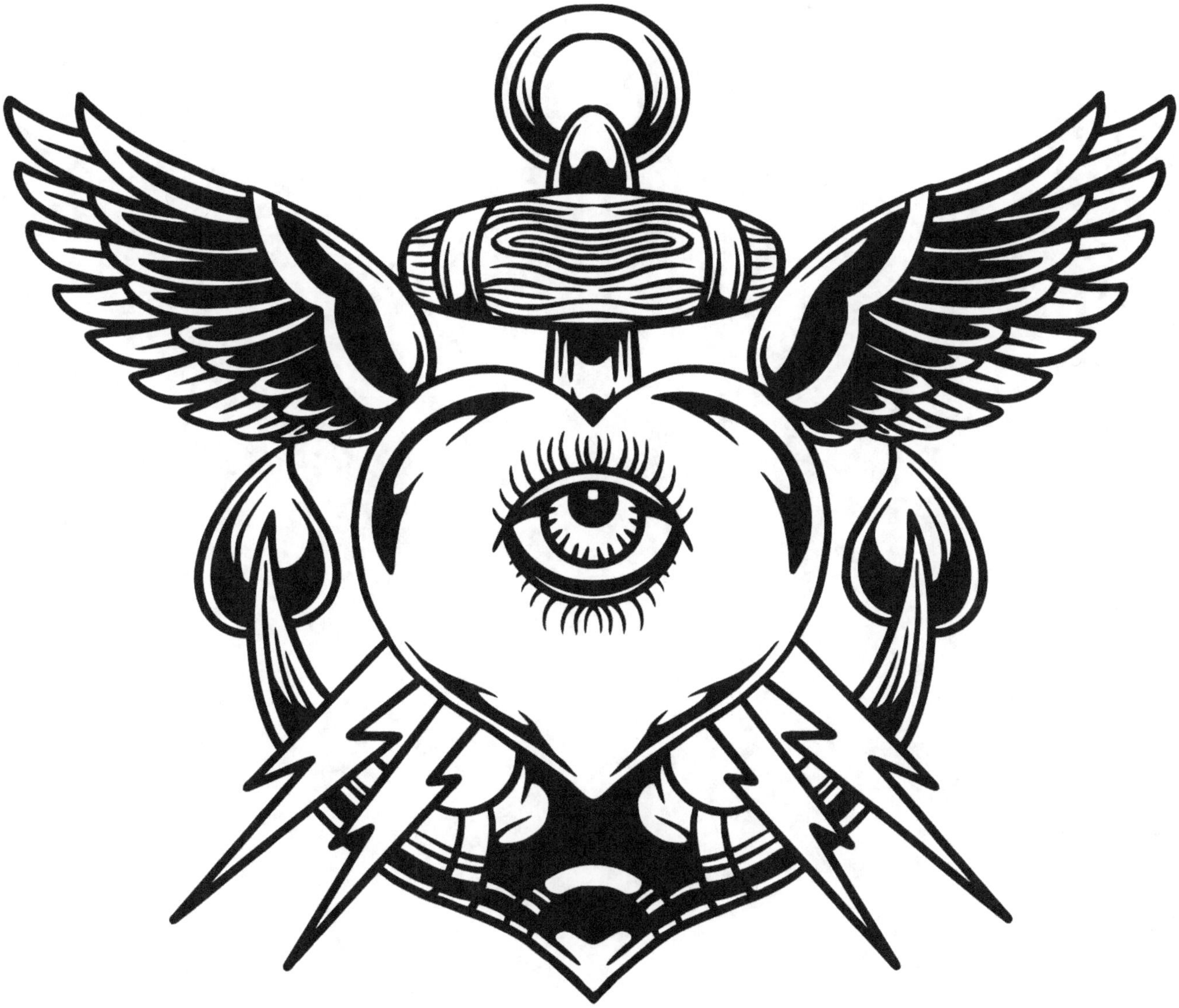

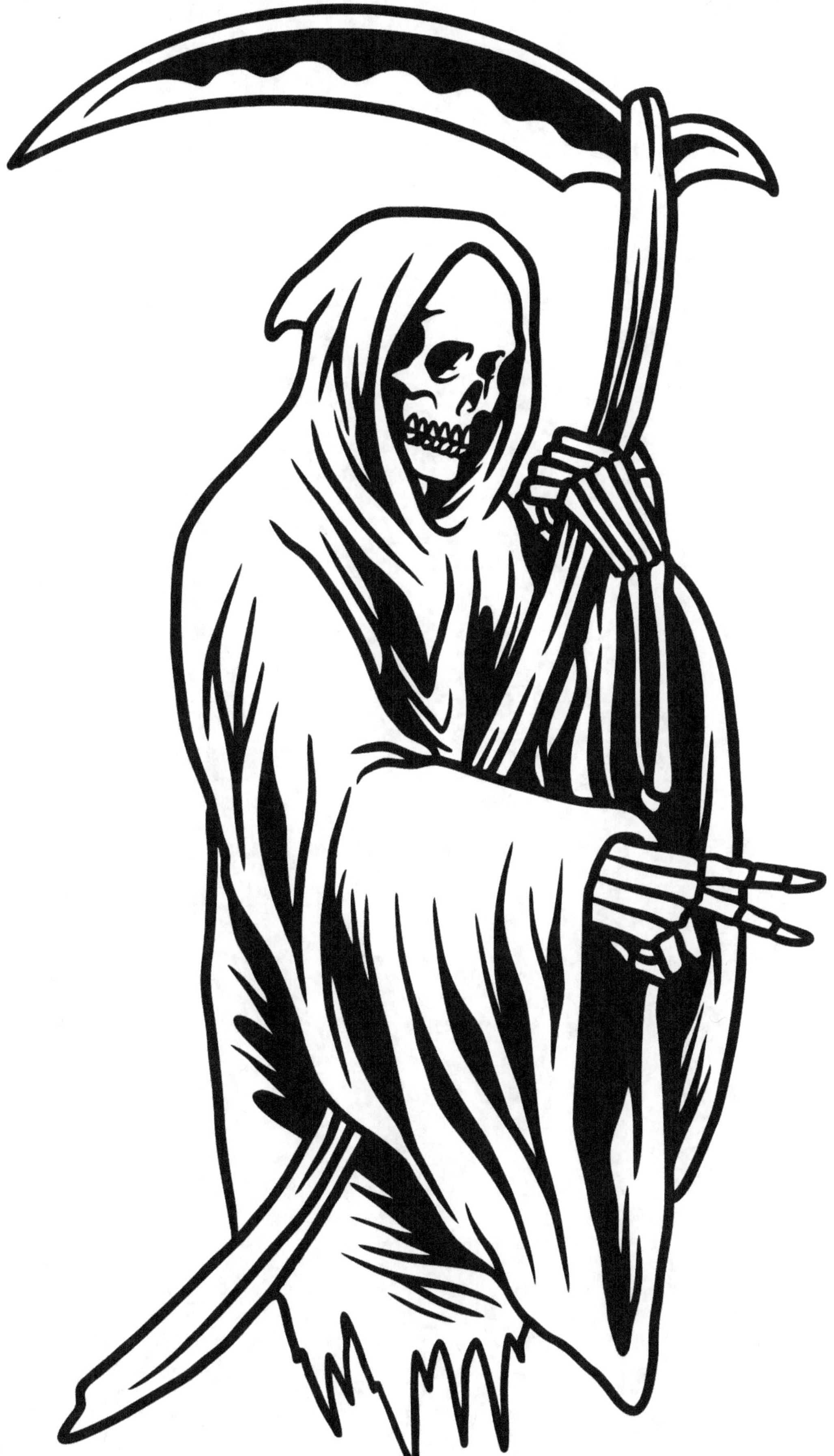

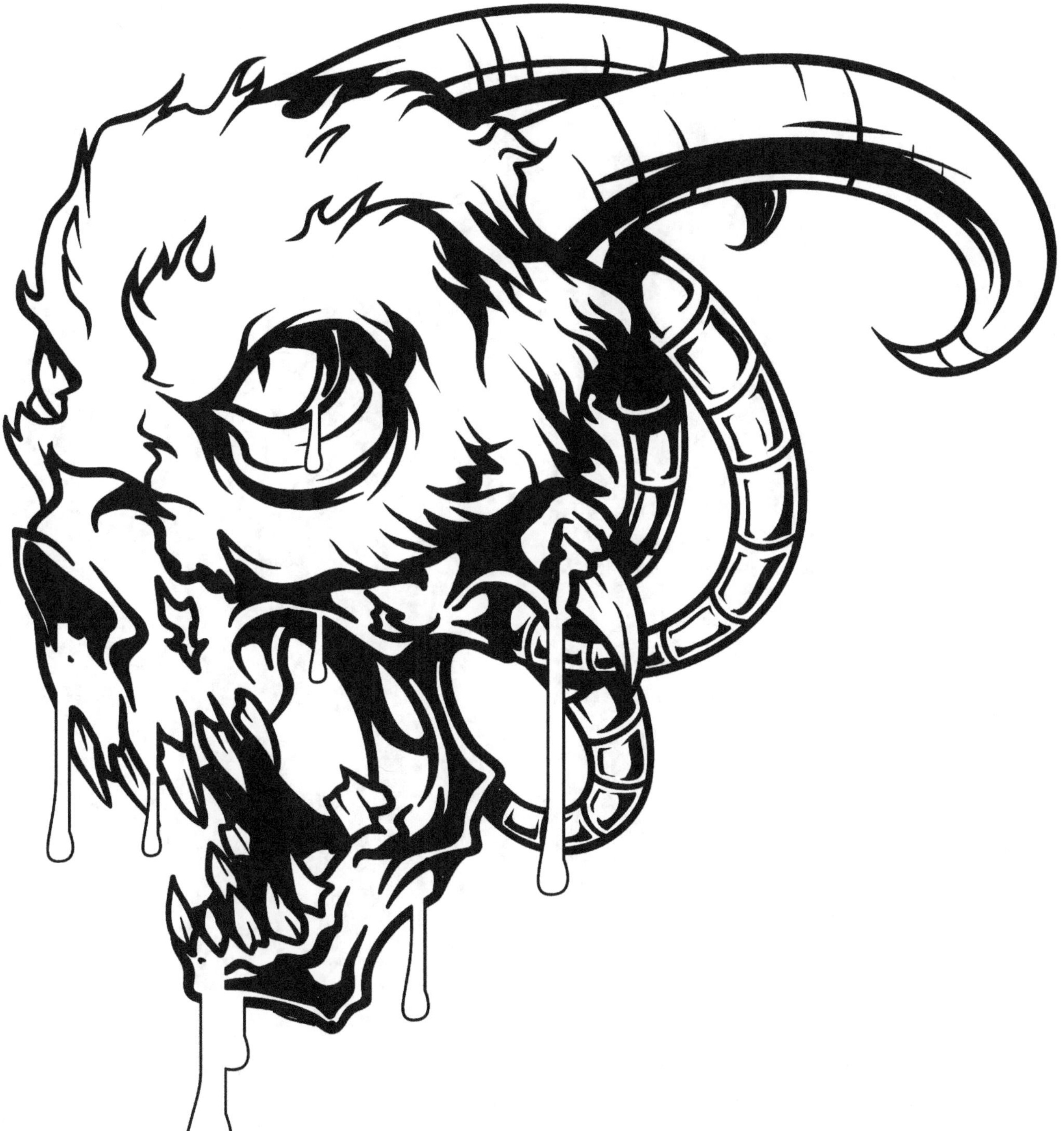

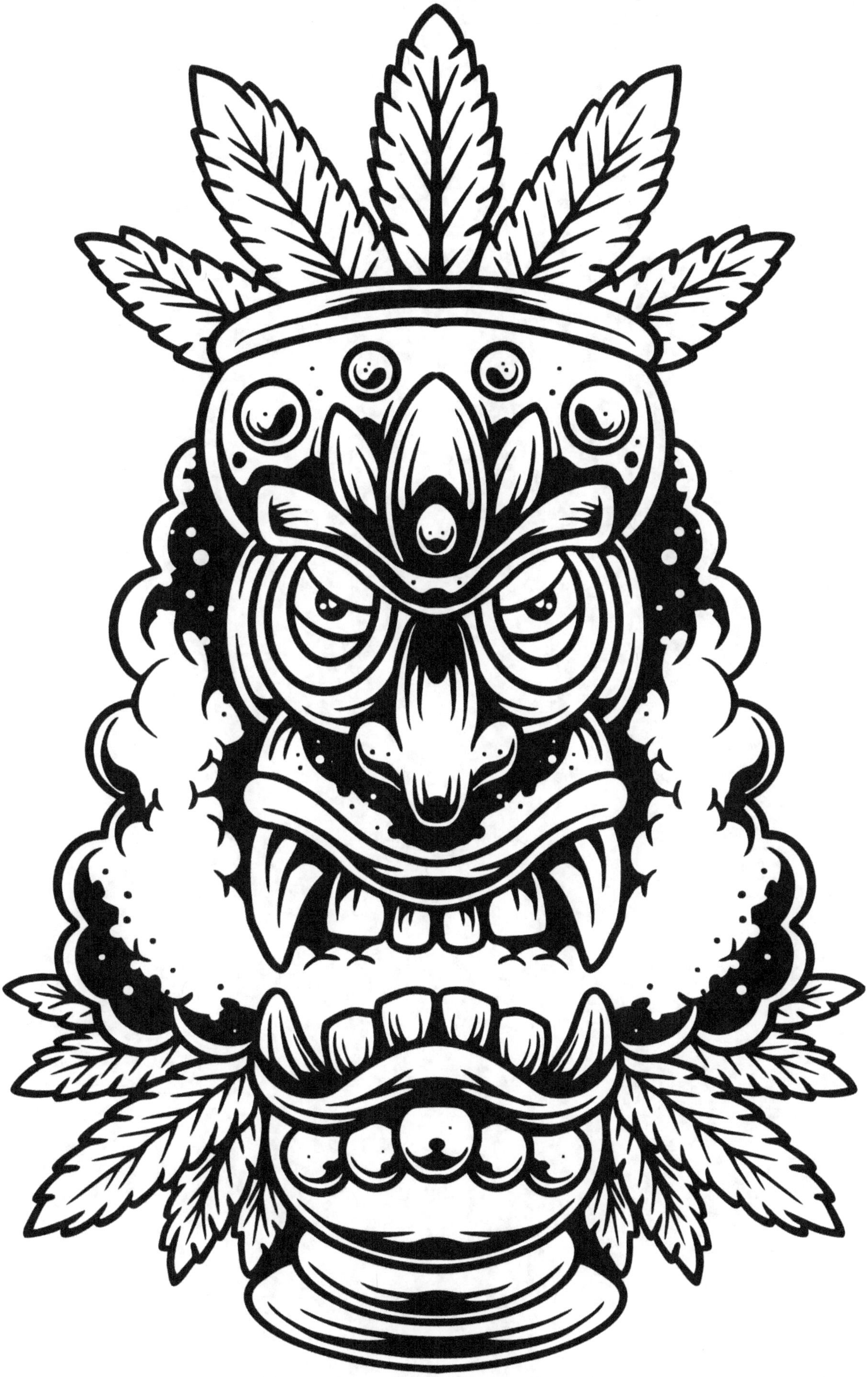

www.ingramcontent.com/pod-product-compliance
Lightning Source LLC
Chambersburg PA
CBHW062358220526
45472CB00008B/1856
9798419585324